Intersecting
Lives:

Road Maps for
Ministry with Young Adults

Dale G. Robinson

Willow City
PRESS

A Ministry
of the
California Southern Baptist Convention

Quotations from *Marketing To Generation X* by Karen Ritchie. Copyright © by Karen Ritchie. Reprinted with permission of The Free Press, a Division of Simon and Schuster.

Quotations reprinted from *Jesus for a New Generation* by Kevin Graham Ford. Copyright © 1995 by Kevin Graham Ford and Jim Denny. Used by permission of InterVaristy Press, P.O. 1400, Downers Grove, Il. 60515.

Quotations from *Sojourners* reprinted with permission from *Sojourners*, 2401 15th St. NW, Washington, D.C.; (202)328-8842/(800)714-7474.

Quotations taken from *Inside the Soul of a New Generation* by Tim Celek and Dieter Zander. Copyright © 1996 by Willow Creek Association. Used by permission of Zondervan Publishing House. Available at your local bookstore or by calling 800-727-3480.

Quotations reprinted from *Generation Next* by George Barna. Copyright © 1995. Regal Books, Ventura, CA 93003. Used by permission.

Quotations reprinted with the permission of Simon & Shuster from *Life after God* by Douglas Coupland. Copyright © 1994 by Douglas Coupland.

Quotations from *Right from Wrong* by Josh McDowell. Copyright © 1994. Used by permission, Word Publishing Company.

Quotations from *Generations: The History of America's Future, 1584 to 2069* by William Strauss and Neil Howe, Copyright © by William Strauss & Neil Howe, by permission of the William Morrow and Company, Inc.

Unless otherwise noted, all scripture quotations are from the NEW AMERICAN STANDARD BIBLE®, Copyright © The Lockman Foundation 1960, 1962, 1963, 1968, 1971, 1972, 1973, 1975, 1977. Used by permission.

Quotations from *The Contemporary English Version of the Bible,* Copyright © 1995, American Bible Society. Used by permission.

ISBN 0-9661778-0-0

First Printing 1998

Library of Congress Catalogue Card Number: 97 62567

Table of Contents

Preface: A Road Well Traveled -------------------------------------- i
Section One: Wayfaring Strangers ------------------------------ 1
Section Two: Intersections --- 7
    1. Humanity
    2. Sexuality
    3. Spirituality
    4. Transition
    5. Culture
    6. Desire
    7. Dynamic Energy

Section Three: The King's Highway --------------------------- 59
    1. The Issue at Hand
        The Great Commission
        Obedience and Disobedience
        From Apathy to Intention
    2. Their Dream Church
        Acceptance
        Separation Yet Inclusion
        Relevance and Excellence
        Vibrant Worship
    3. The Specifics
    4. Starting Points for the Church

Section Four: The Leader's Map Book ----------------------- 68
    Route 1: Heart
    Route 2: Character
    Route 3: Discernment
    Route 4: Wisdom
    Route 5: Conduct
    Route 6: Technique
    Route 7: Balance

Section Five: Hazards on the Ministry Highway ------------- 123
    1. False Impressions
    2. Ministry in the Smaller Church
    3. Age Differences in Young Adults
    4. Married Young Adults
    5. Single Young Adults with Children
    6. Working with Church Staff
    7. Inter-Church Cooperation

Section Six: Different Makes and Models --------------------- 133
    1. Suburban Intersections: Young Adult Ministry at
       First Baptist, Poway
    2. Reversing the Trend: Young Adult Ministry at Concord
       Korean Baptist Church
    3. Crossing Our Cultural Borders: Young Adult Ministry
       at Primera Iglesia Bautista del Sur
    4. Pathways of Ministry: Young Adult Ministry at St.
       Stephen Baptist Church
Appendices --- 169

    1. Resources
    2. Suggested Topics and Issues
    3. Outreach Ideas

Bibliography -- 177

To Betty, for the best years.

Preface

A Road Well Traveled

I regularly travel the length of California. I can navigate Highway 99 blindfolded. The twists and turns of the Los Angeles freeway system are familiar acquaintances, as are the "shortcuts" across the high desert. I love driving Pacific Coast Highway, but only some portions of Highway 1, and never from Mill Valley to Stinson Beach. I fear the Sacramento freeways, and those in downtown L.A., but think the 14 from Mojave to Lancaster is great. My car and I have found ourselves parked on the ribbon parking lot known as Interstate 405. We have pushed the speed-limit envelope on freeway and two-lane alike.

I recognize my travels as a metaphor for life which also consists of starts and stops, turns and straight-aways, speed and parking, hassle-free driving and shredded tires. Sometimes the road is a superhighway. Other times it is bumpy or nearly non-existent. The journey continues. I am always on the road of life, and I am not alone.

Everyone else is traveling too. We do not all travel the same roads, or start the journey at the same time. Yet, the roads of our lives intersect repeatedly. This is true for individuals and for groups. This is especially true of those of us with the fish symbol pasted to our rear bumpers.

Knowing Jesus adds new dimension to life's journey. This relationship gives believers a divine purpose: to share the Good News. It is to tell about the great narrow, but high, Way on which the

King bids us travel. We seek to intersect the lives of non-believers so that they too may find a new spiritual interstate prepared for God's own travel.

My journey has taken me many places. Interestingly, I seem always to be intersecting the lives of a certain group of people, young adults, 18-28 or 30 years of age. I first learned the good that comes from this meeting of lives as God intersected mine through devout Sunday School teachers, pastors and campus ministers. I experienced that goodness again as I touched the lives of young Filipino college students, and later on as I worked with junior college students in Texas. I then took a different road that had me working with campus ministers and the church's ministry with young adults. Throughout those years I learned how one brief episode of the Gospel crossing paths with a young adult life changed that life for eternity. I saw young adults grow up to become leaders and spiritual examples in their own right.

Intersecting young adults for Jesus' sake is simple obedience to the Great Commission. It is the church's opportunity, one of the grandest in all of its travels, to contact and change the lives of an entire generation.

This effort at providing road maps for ministry to young adults could not have happened without the influence and effort of many individuals. I want to acknowledge the influence and help of the following persons: Dr. Bill Hogue, Dr. Mike Miller, Dr. Montia Setzler, Dr. Fermín Whittaker, Mr. Tim Cleary, Mrs. Christy Haines, Members of the 1995 Jenness Park Focus Group, Sabina Butler, Jason D. Robinson, Randall D. Robinson and Nathan Brown.

I deeply appreciate the technical assistance of my secretary, Debbie Araujo, and my colleagues, Beth Bush and Terry Barone.

Section One

Wayfaring Strangers

*"A generation goes, and a generation comes,
but the earth remains forever."*
Ecclesiastes 1:4

The impetus for this book came at the intersection of professional crisis and personal trauma. I felt I had been run over by the proverbial eighteeen wheeler. A financial crisis in our denomination necessitated the elimination of the salaried campus ministry positions in our state. This was a personal trauma because I was required to tell friends and colleagues that their jobs were going to disappear. It was a ministerial crisis in that I was forced to rethink, not my calling, but my style and approach to ministry.

When the dust cleared, I discovered a new system of opportunities opening for me and for young adults. I found that there were thousands of young adults in our churches needing assistance and encouragement. I discovered that churches needed to be challenged to minister to young adults and leaders needed training.

As one ministry highway closed, a new one opened. I was free to work with local church ministries with young adults, and champion young adult causes. I began a new phase as a kind of road warrior for young adults. This book is an outgrowth of that part of my pilgrimage. It is an attempt to help churches, church leaders and Sunday School teachers begin at the beginning. The challenge is to help them face the realities of working with young adults. It is an attempt to affirm those already working with young adults, and to prepare those who want to begin this working with them.

Two Premises

There are two basic premises which undergird the content of this book. They inform everything I have written here.

Premise #1

One of the few universal experiences of humanity is the aging process. Every child will most likely be 18, or 20, or 30. Every adult has at one time been 18, or 20, or 30. Every adult knows, though some have forgotten, the challenges of those first, stumbling, adult years. Every person moves through the stages of life, and in so doing shares a variety of common basic experiences. People really are more alike than different.

We see persons first, and generations second. Only the year on the calendar, the styles we affect or the events of history are different. Journeys keep beginning and roads keep crossing. That knowledge undergirds the first premise of this book: <u>universal principles, issues and transitions apply to all 18-28 year olds regardless of date of birth</u>.

While the current young adult generation is unique to its own time and experiences, it has many features in common with both its predecessors and its successors. Along with their uniqueness, it is those places where their life journeys intersect our own that we wish to understand. As the church corporately and individually, we have a real reason to move our lives in their direction and so intersect with them. Jesus is our reason, and their salvation is our purpose.

Premise #2

Much has been said about generational sociology and dynamics. It is important to understand those dynamics. They help us comprehend why, to continue our metaphor, some groups or generations drive big, powerful cars in the fast lane at 30 m.p.h., and others drive four-cylinder compact cars at 90 m.p.h., winding through traffic. They help us know why some people have sports cars and others have minivans.

In these waning years of the twentieth century one generation of adults begins to think about the garage; another is just starting its engines. A new crop of young adults makes itself felt on the world scene. New adults, born anytime after 1961, are embarking on their life journeys. They are ubiquitous, filling up our colleges, serving our hamburgers, and sometimes leading our communities and churches. Several million strong, they bear many names. "Twentysomethings," "13ers," "Busters," "Slackers," "Generation X," the "Invisible Generation," "Generation Y," "Generation Next," are among the commonest, and most detested.[1]

Their unique experiences have led to the second premise for this project: <u>the church best serves young adults by understanding their spiritual needs.</u> To reach young adults it will learn about the forces that shape their lives. It will intentionally seek to cross paths with them. It will recognize that there are differences between "them" and "us." It will understand that those differences must be addressed if we are to gain a hearing for the claims of the Gospel. The young adult of the 90's has had different shaping experiences than the young adults of the 60's, 70's and 80's. Those experiences have shaped their attitudes and feelings, and needs. In response the church will intentionally seek to intersect their lives.

A Word to Those in the Driver's Seat

I want to affirm those who work with young adults through the church. Truly, you do real work when you cross roads with young adults. Because it is real work, you need to understand their life situations, developmental issues and transitions. You need this understanding to have healthy relationships with them as persons; to develop realistic expectations of those relationships; and to know what your work with them will accomplish. This understanding is necessary so you won't burn out from the heightened frustrations of this intense people work.

Young adults are sinful persons going through multiples of life transitions in a short time. Cultural circumstances shape their perceptions of reality, truth and morals. Struggling with a feeling of "almost, but not quite," they desire relationships that enhance their self-worth and recognize them as full-fledged adults. Dynamic and powerful, they have much to offer God, the church, and society. They are an "army" ready to mobilize. This first section identifies those who will benefit the most from reading this book. It sets out its premises and describes its organization.

The second section will focus on the intersections where the Gospel can touch their lives. These are the points where this generation's life experience crosses ours. Those seven common intersections are: humanity, spirituality, sexuality, transition, culture, desire and dynamic energy.

The third section will examine the elements for creating a young-adult friendly church. To find this out we asked young adults what they looked for in a church. Their answers clue us into the kind of environment church leaders need to stimulate to involve young adults.

The fourth section will deal with the character traits required of those who work and minister with young adults. These are the traits that need special attention and cultivation if the ministry is to be successful.

Section five is a travel planning guide for leadership. It suggests some of the real or imagined hazards we encounter in traveling down the road.

In the final section, representative leaders from various types of churches will describe their ministries. They will suggest ways to minister to young adults in their cultural contexts and reflect on the unique needs of the young adults with whom they work.

[1]William Strauss and Neil Howe, Generations: A History of America's Future. (New York: William Morrow, 1991), pp. 30-32. Kent Jones, "Talkin' 'bout our generation," Seventeen, August 1993, p. 131. George Barna, The Invisible Generation: Baby Busters. (Glendale, CA: The Barna Research Group, Ltd., 1992) pp. 18-23.

Section Two

Intersections

"And the Lord said to the servant, go out into the highways and hedges, and compel them to come in, that my house may be filled."
Luke 14:23 (KJV)

Intersections are those common spaces two roads share when they cross. Look at them one way and they belong to one road. See them from a different angle and they belong to the other. People's paths cross in those intersections everyday, every hour, and even every minute. Usually this happens without incident. Sometimes, however, the physical law that objects can not occupy the same place at the same time comes into play and crashes happen. Then things get really interesting!

Human lives intersect like roads. For brief moments two or more lives share the same space and interact. They have common ground. These are the points and the times lives can be touched and changed. We have identified seven such intersections.

Intersection Number One:
Humanity

While it may be obvious, it is necessary to assert that young adults are human. There seems to be some thinking "out there" that labels them some kind of sub, or super-human race. Our culture has made a cult of youth, giving it a veneer of Greek-like idealism. Youth, and young sex, are marketing ploys for everything from faucets to deodorant. We glamorize youth to the point of forgetting their diverse humanity. We have forgotten that youth is fleeting. Yet, the first intersection for believers and young adults is their common humanity.

The Image of God

The grand Biblical truth about our shared humanity is that God's image is at the core of every person's being. Scripture is explicit. Genesis 1:27 recounts concerning Father Adam and Mother Eve: "And God created man in His own image, in the image of God He created him; male and female He created them." All humanity carries within it this image. We bear the marks of being God's creation, an uncanny resemblance to our Heavenly Father.

Of what does this image consist? Certainly it is nothing physical. Few, if any of us, can truly claim to look "godlike." If we do think so, all we have to do is wait a few years and that illusion will disappear. The image of God exists as the basic human abilities that separate us from the animals: the power to reason, think, choose, exercise free will, love unconditionally, overcome instinct and even habit. These things, plus the ability to respond to a loving Heavenly Father, constitute the image of God.

Young adults, as human as they come, are inheritors of this same image. It marks them as blatantly as any tattoo. It is more permanent, impervious even to the laser light of God's own stare.

Sinful

It may seem negative to define young adults as sinful. They may consider it a judgmental put-down, an attack on their worth as persons. Some of their detractors may use this term to attack and damage their self-esteem. Biblically, however, sinfulness is no judgment on their human worth. It is a statement of a universal spiritual rebellion against a loving God. It is a status unifying them with everyone else.[1]

The Scriptures teach that rebellious humanity is a fallen race. As such, each person is a fallen creature. This is who we are as humans. We are sinners by nature and by choice. When given the options, we choose rebellion and sin. We replay Adam and Eve's sin on a daily, even hourly, basis. There is no doubt about it. We human beings are "guilty as sin."[2]

Having long since moved from new-born innocence, young adults know right from wrong. They struggle with moral choices their parents and grandparents would swoon imagining. They willfully, often and sometimes with great glee, rebel against all they know as moral. Each and every one feels the pull of lust, jealousy, anger, rebellion. If they are unsaved, they need salvation. Romans 3:23 (KJV), "For all have sinned, and come short of the glory of God," applies to them as to anyone. If they are believers, they need the daily touch (some would say *kick in the pants*) of God's ongoing grace. Just as they need physical and social maturity, they need spiritual maturity.

The bottom line is that young adults are eminently human. Their souls are permeated by a predisposition to rebellion against God. They are human because, even sinful, they are saveable. God's mercy has provided a "way of escape" from the consequences of sin in the Person of Jesus Christ. We can understand young adults only as we see them through God's eyes, as dying sinners sought relentlessly by His saving grace.

Intersection Number Two:
Sexuality

The college sophomore son is calling. The voice is choked and strained. The silences are long. He drops the ax: "Dad, my girlfriend is pregnant, and we are getting married next month." An impulsive sexual decision changes everyone's lives.

That real-life experience highlights young adult sexuality. They are first known by gender, then by name. By age 18 they are well-experienced in the urges of sexual maturity. Every moment, every thought, every relationship, feels its influence. They move through a hormone-drenched adolescence to a hormone-saturated adulthood.

Young adults act on their sexuality, making virginity a scarce commodity. Recent studies describe a general population in which 81% of 20 year old unmarried males and 67% of 20 year old unmarried females have already had sexual intercourse. Cohabitation before marriage is a common practice.[3]

Christian young adults seem no different. Sexual activity within that group almost matches that of the general population. Christian author, Josh McDowell interviewed 3,795 church-going teenagers 11-18 years of age. Of that group 15% had had sexual intercourse, (the 17-18 year age group rose to 27%), and 55% admitted to some kind of overt sexual behavior in the three months prior to the survey. In the collision of hormones and religious values, hormones have the upper hand. [4]

It is not sufficient to merely recognize young adults as sexual beings. We must discover how to intersect them with the Gospel. To do that requires an understanding of that sexuality.

First, Sexuality is at the heart of their humanity. It is as much a reflection of God's image as free will and intelligence. The guilt that must inevitably come when sex is misused is a result of their fallen and sinful natures.

Second, young adults act on their sexuality because society has lowered the standards. They experience few powerful role models of sexual purity. Their homes often have none. Certainly, television promotes none.

Third, sex seems a means of acquiring what the love, affection, security, caring, family they lacked as children. Whether sex can provide those things is questionable. Yet, that is where they look.

Fourth, the rise of AIDS and other sexually transmitted diseases has made sex a risky business. The question for this generation is not whether sexual intercourse is right, but whether it is worth the hassle. Yet they do it anyway, the element of risk adding a bit of spice to the adventure.[5]

Their sexuality impacts them, for good or ill. They must cope with the issues, concerns, and problems it raises. To understand their intense sexuality is to begin to understand them. To share the Gospel of grace and forgiveness with them at the point of their guilt, and personal need is to begin to bring redemption to their lives.[6]

Intersection Number Three:
Spirituality

In the company of countless others
we search for eternal truth, integrity
and embrace the struggle, the love.

I want to be faithful, I want to be courageous,
I want to shoulder up and shake the world,
I want to pray, I want to see God.[7]

Outsiders observing young adults might scoff at the claims that they are spiritual. Their music, life, and dress paint them a dark, secular black. Yet, spirituality may be the deepest motivator of this group. They give every indication of having a "hunger and thirst after righteousness," of seeking inner wholeness, spiritual wellness, integrity, reconciliation, and unity with God.[8] They seem to be seeking something to give life structure, solidity, and meaning. This meaningfulness may come from values or ethics. For others it may be philosophy or eastern religions. For others, it may be some sense of individual worth, or a vague notion of goodness.[9]

Douglas Coupland, an unofficial spokesperson for this generation, describes his feelings this way:

I think the price we paid for our golden life was an inability to fully believe in love; instead we gained an irony that scorched everything it. But then I must remind myself we are living creatures, that we have religious impulses—we must—and yet into what cracks do these impulses flow in a world without religion? It is something I think about every day. Sometimes I think it is the only thing I should be thinking about.

Now here is my secret: I tell it to you with an openness of heart that I doubt I shall ever achieve again, so I pray that you are in a quiet room as you hear these words. My secret is that I need God—that I am sick and can no longer make it alone. I need God to help me give, because I no longer seem capable of giving; to help me be kind, as I no longer seem capable of kindness; to help me love, as I seem beyond being able to love.[10]

A Yearning for God

This generation has an ill-defined yearning for God. It comes more intensely to them because they know suffering. They experienced the vacuum caused by family tragedy, breakup, abuse or economic hardship. They have shared it with their friends as they experienced personal hurt. They have watched it vicariously as CNN reflected real life pain in Somalia or some inner city, or as MTV has reflected the exaggerated anguish of "The Real World."

They yearn for God because they have an intimate acquaintance with loneliness. From early childhood, young adults came home to empty houses, or broken relationships. They often had to make do with their own companionship or with people who really were not family. Because they know loneliness, they seek to find community and family, even spiritual family.

Young adults seek God because, whether they realize it or not, they need forgiveness. They need a spiritual release from the real or self-imposed guilt that infects their lives. They tried sex, and found it empty. Frantically, they seek to fill the guilty vacancies of life.

The love of God can fill their spiritual vacuum. The Gospel, mediated by loving believers, can introduce young adults to the redemption they so radically need. Agape love can open the closed doors of suffering, aloneness and guilt.[11]

A Rejection of Organized Religion
Corporately, their spirituality is a quest for God, not necessarily a quest for orthodox Christianity. The irony is that while young adulthood is an intense time of spiritual seeking, it is the time of least church involvement.[12]

This is an acute problem for the church. Nearly 80% of persons in church youth groups jump ship after high school graduation. They disappear from Bible study and worship. They are "out there." On one side, churches that have high profile youth groups do little or nothing long term for their graduates. The churches essentially abandon young adults. On the other, the young adults themselves have a natural tendency to move on.[13]

The church is guilty. Think about it. A typical church spends significant dollars annually on youth ministry, focusing on 7th-12th graders. They honor them. They encourage them. They send them on mission trips, choir trips, and youth conferences. Even the smallest church has a youth class, a teacher and concerned parents.

After high school graduation the situation changes. Zap! Nothing! The youth group tolerates those recent graduates for a while, but eventually loses interest in them. Life also pulls them away from the youth, as high school fades, and from church as work and play intervene. The church's negligence also factors in. It has not provided for young adults in Sunday School. Neither has it taught its youth to anticipate continued participation in a dynamic college-career group.

Fallout For A Reason

While the church is guilty of dumping their graduates unceremoniously into adulthood, it is not at fault for young adult fall out. Young adults drop out because of personal transitions as much as the lack of church ministry for them. Researchers have discovered at least four reasons why young adults move away from church involvement.

First, the development of critical thinking skills calls all previously held, personally untested beliefs into question. Combined with a developing sense that "everything, including truth, is relative" often makes the absoluteness of the claims of Christ unattractive.

Second, the development of sexuality leads to behavior the church considers inappropriate. That produces a sense of guilt for participating. Since young adults cannot handle guilt, or at least being confronted by it, they will avoid the place where they feel the most guilty, the church.

Third, as they strive to be physically independent, they may have abandoned church. They no longer "have to" go and so they do not. For many, it is a remnant of an oppressive childhood, a husk they can quickly discard.

Fourth, they can move beyond parental control by moving away from their parents' church. This affirms and confirms their independence, and clarifies, if only for themselves, their adulthood.[14]

While these four reasons are valid, they cannot tell the entire story. Free will, conflict with parents, and even the influence of girl friends or boy friends can impact church involvement. The factors listed are influential, but not determinative. If young adults decide to involve themselves, they will, but they have to have a reason.

Intersection Number Four: *Transitions*

On-ramps and Lane changes

Freeway driving takes practice. You need a combination of guts and grace to brave big city traffic at rush hour, or any hour for that matter. You have to be constantly aware of your location related to the off-ramp you want to take, and be ready to transition left or right to get there. Sometimes you have no choice but to move over when the lane suddenly disappears. Sometimes you gasp in fear as that other fellow suddenly and dangerously cuts you off to change lanes, or weaves in and out of traffic. You nearly have heart failure when that sports car ahead of you flips on his blinker and dashes across three lanes of traffic to make the off-ramp. All that happens before you get to the downtown interchange, where it is really dangerous!

Life for young adults is much like that freeway. It consists of traffic, crowded lanes, hazards and a great number of lane changes. Those transitions come because nature or society forces them upon young adults. They constantly find themselves in "lane ends, merge left, merge right" situations not of their own making, but which they must navigate to survive.

Older adults understand these life transitions. They are veterans. Young adults do not. The trauma and intensity of transition take its toll, pushing them to behaviors running the gamut from mildly weird to clearly aberrational. Changes in their emotions, physical appearance, or life situations come in rapid fire order. There is little time to assimilate recent lane changes before new ones demand their attention. All the changes are confusing, yet they are foundations for the rest of life. From them spring all the attitudes, goals and directions of a constantly transforming adulthood.[15]

If lane changes on crowded freeways can unnerve the most experienced driver, think of what those physical, emotional, social and spiritual transitions can do to a young adult. Just as changing lanes is a natural part of driving, so these transitions make up the fabric of adulthood. Because they are being "shaken up" by these experiences, they are more receptive to the friendly "other guy" who gives way or helps them. While there are many changes they experience, six emerge as the most prevalent. These are the basic ones, crucial to their "driving" skills. These transitions have to do with their minds, their relationships with other people and God, their place in society and their outlook on life.

#1: From Concrete to Abstract Reasoning

Drastic changes take place in a person's thinking ability between 17 and 24 years of age. Young teenagers are concrete thinkers, able to understand only the boldest and most obvious facts. As they mature, they develop the ability to think in abstract terms. It is like a flower opening as they discover their ability to comprehend the reasons behind the rules, or the nature of love, or the person of God. They discover they can reason things out.

One of their major developmental tasks is learning to make appropriate decisions based on the facts, circumstances, and sound advice. This increase in critical thinking abilities is most intense at age 18 and 19, or during the freshman year of college.[16]

#2: From Simple to Complex Relationships

Becoming an adult involves new and unfolding relationships, a process with anxiety and insecurity. Everyone involved has to be flexible and open to the changes.

a) Relationships with the Opposite Sex

During late adolescence males and females begin to see each other in new light. The need for intimacy, the male-female bond and marriage becomes more evident. This transformation has as many opportunities for failure as it does for success. There is still the intense game playing and rivalry of the dating world, but there is also a change in tone. Young men begin seriously to consider finding a mate, or at least become more open to the possibility. Casual dating relationships have a new intensity, as they become mating dances. Young women continue the quest begun long ago, with a little more sophistication.

This is no headlong plunge into marital permanency, though that is part of the mix. Young adults are waiting longer to marry than in the past. [17] The need for career training and personal development sometimes makes spouse-seeking a lower priority. The transformation comes when young adults need to understand the nature of relationships, and begin to see member of the opposite gender as worthy of close personal relationship, rather than as objects for personal gratification.

b) Interpersonal Relationships

Each young adult must adjust to new relationships with persons of the same gender. High school and college provide opportunities for brotherhood and sisterhood like no other time in life. These are times of focus on male or female friends. This is a valuable time, for it is in these groups of same gender friends, that young adults work out their course of life action, and cast their dreams

for the future. These are times solidifying roles in a safe and secure environment.[18]

#3: From Dependence to Independence

Have you ever seen a ship leaving the dock? At first it is secured to
the relative safety of the dock by hawsers of stout knotted rope.
Then, as the vessel starts its engines, it pulls away. Crew unhooks
the lines one at a time until the ship is launched. It is then ready to
get under way. Departure is risk and adventure. Moving under its
own power the vessel casts away its secure shore ties and moves
into dangerous seas.

Young adults inescapably experience that kind of letting go.
Whether they realize it or not, they are moving more and more
under their own power. They travel away from the security of
home and high school to the insecure waters of the real world,
seeking employment, and starting education all over again.

a) Relating to Parents

Young adulthood continues and intensifies that process that began at birth, the making of the new child into an autonomous
person. The transition to autonomy is a rocky process. Parents
want to let go, but cannot. They sabotage their children's effort
at independence, sometimes unconsciously, and at other times
on purpose. This separating time places parents in their own dilemma. A grown-up child means an aging parent. Suddenly, "their
baby" is acting much too independently. It can be as difficult and
crucial a time for the parent as for the child.

If parents are too smothering, they risk losing a new adult friend.
They risk developing an unhealthy co-dependency. If they are too
free, loose or adversarial, they risk the same thing. During this
transition, parents must choose the middle way of intentional

adult development. They must give their child more freedom, and responsibility, and must continue and consistently communicate with them. Treat that young adult as an adult, and he or she will act like one. Help them experience first hand the Siamese twins of freedom and responsibility. The end result will be well-adjusted young adults who see their parents both as parents and as friends, allies in the struggle for adulthood.

b) Relating to Money and Finances

Young adults are still financially dependent on their parents. Their earning power does not match their desire for acquisition. Their goal is to become financially independent or at least less dependent. It is a slow process. [19]

Their own mixed emotions transfix them like deer in the headlights. On one hand the ropes of finances, debt, and earning power still tightly strap them to their parents. On the other hand, they want to be "on their own." They want adult things and possessions yet cannot obtain and sustain them. Young adulthood is a time when others push and encourage then to move from dependent child to independent adult. The tension comes when this does not happen soon enough for either the parent or the young adult.

c) Relating to Society

At age 18 and high school graduation, society begins to expect different things of them. They are "legally of age," a status that brings both privileges and liabilities. They can to vote and be drafted into the armed services. If they break the law, they face stiffer adult penalties. Automobile insurance discriminates against them, causing a major drain on their finances. One day, they will have to file their income tax. Inevitably they transition to new roles and responsibilities in society.

d) Relating to Self-image

Their self image is changing. They understand what it means to be a "little kid," but are having to work through the issues of being adult. They are trying to figure out how "real" adults act and interact. The process of self-image or identity development will result in a full grown adult. It is a process in which these young adults solidify their self-image and gain confidence, self-awareness and boldness.[20]

The difficulty comes in determining exactly what are the characteristics of real men and women. The options are legion. Young adults will try or contemplate a variety of behaviors, some of which would scandalize their parents. Ultimately a pattern of adult behavior emerges. Though tentative at first, young adults will define for themselves what it means to be a man or a woman. The outcome is vital, however. How they deal with the self-image issue will determine the kind of husband, wife, father, mother they will become. It will determine the shape of the rest of their lives.

#4: From Security to Adventure

It was the second week of school and the college freshmen had begun to locate their classes, the cafeteria, the student center and the library. Now it was time to give attention to the buildings on the edges of campus. There was one that was especially intriguing. Its sign said, "Baptist Student Center, Everyone Welcome." Did it mean it was for Baptists, but that anyone could come too? The college freshman would just have to find out. So, the freshman went up to the door, intent on going in. Then, anxiety hit. "What if they did not want freshmen to come in, or what if no one speaks to me? What will happen when I go in?" Timidly, the freshman opens the door. What happens next depends on the freshman. If she is shy, a greeting from students already in the lounge could frighten her off. If she is even a *little bit adventurous, she might go in and discover a whole new set of friends.*

This little drama of life, the freshman discovering the Baptist students center, is a parable of the transformation from security to adventure. High school graduation is a high moment, followed by a slow realization that a drastic change has taken place. They lose a position of identity and security. Though they don't know it yet, high school graduation broke their safety zones, and comfort groups. Just like Humpty Dumpty, those securities can never to be put back together again. The passage from required formal to elective discretionary education or the real world is rocky indeed.

a) New Relationships for Old

First, there is the steady erosion of relationships with old high school friends. The bonds that held the group together stretch to the breaking point. Some go to colleges. Some get jobs that demand their time. Common interests and involvements no longer exist. The breakup of "the old gang" moves along inevitably. There arises the need for new friends, for a realignment of relationships.

b) Graduation

Graduation brings change in social status. Once they were high and mighty seniors, now they find their place taken by the has-been junior, now in place senior class. They are "out," and no one really wants them around anymore. No longer honored as high achievers, they are lucky if someone yells, "Hey you, Mr. Drive Up Window, I need an order of fries." They have tumbled from being an honored leader to something less than the scum of the earth; from mighty senior, a "less than zero" nobody. "How the mighty have fallen!"

It is as if someone tossed them into the deep end before they really learned to swim. Amazingly, after a few sputtering moments, they begin to swim. They make some remarkable discoveries about themselves and their abilities. Yes, they face an insecure future after the comfort of high school, but now they have to function on their own. They revel in their new found ability and skill. Each young adult says to himself, "Yes, I can do something on my own. I am forced to. They have pushed me out of the nest. So, like the commercial says, I'll 'just do it'."

#5: From Family Religion to Personal Faith

Research shows that evangelical churches have a retention rate of only 20% of their high school graduates.[21] This is a reflection of the churches' own strategic intention to reach young adults, or lack of it. More importantly, however, it is an indication of the turmoil young adults experience about their religious faith. On the one hand, they find themselves uncomfortable or resistant to the faith of their childhood. On the other, they know they are in spiritual need, and yearn for a personal sense of something to fill that God-shaped void in their lives.

a) Mature Questing and Real Decisions

Coming of age involves the freedom to decide and live with the consequences. Because they can question, they will. They will investigate, evaluate and challenge old notions and new facts. Nothing is off-limits. Nothing is untouchable. Perhaps this new questioning is due to a growing maturity. Perhaps it is due to a reaction of their formal education with their religious heritage. Perhaps it is due to some kind of mystical, eye-opening experience regarding parental religion. Regardless of its origin, young adults will question the religion of their childhood, and seek to find a faith of their own.[22]

b) Just Because Momma Went to Church

Many young adults must deal with the fact that they grew up in a certain religious context. It may be intense and active. It may be nominal or cultural. It may be hostile or even non-religious. It is this context, regardless of its religious intensity, which young adults will question.

Sometimes, they are Baptist or Catholic or Presbyterian because that is their family or national identity. So, whether or not they remain active in a church, they always claim to be one or the other. In many instances it is a cultural identity. They are (you name the church) only, and merely, because Mamma, Papa and all the Grandparents belong there.

Sometimes, they are believers, dedicated to God's service. These young adults may not question the bed-rock beliefs of the faith. They likely will challenge the style, ambiance, organization and even the content of their home church. They will be open to attending different churches in the ever-present search for relationship, acceptance and an acceptable intellectual content.

c) Taking Jesus as My Savior

Young adults are making life-shaping decisions and solidifying attitudes that will impact the rest of their lives.[23] Their baby faith, such as they have, is being tried in the fire. It will emerge refined or burnt up. It is the time of real decision. They will either accept Jesus as Savior and Lord or cast Him aside as just another parental ghost to be ignored.

#6: From Idealism to Realism

Some time during early adolescence mental lights turn on. In young adulthood those lights get brighter and brighter. Clouded reality becomes more brightly exposed the older one gets. As a result, they can see people, situations, circumstances as those things really are. The development of critical thinking skills moves this along. New understanding and perceptions of reality cause an awakening of the senses. Reality transforms as experience removes the rose-colored glasses of a protected life. The real world bulges in. A long, dry summer of disillusionment begins.

They learned long ago who the Tooth Fairy, the Easter Bunny and Santa Claus really were. Now they realize that neither parent is God or Superman, but only human. Teachers, youth leaders and pastors lose their aura of semi-divinity. What heroes they have topple from feet of clay. This new awareness is not just because young adults are becoming more discerning, but also because older adults act in sinful ways young adults recognize.

Disillusionment is almost a rite of passage, a required step on the path to adulthood. It is like having a bucket of ice cold water thrown on your head when you realize just how mistaken you were about parents and life. No one escapes it. All must respond to it. Some succumb to bitterness, and develop a cold cynicism about the world. Others retreat to sentimentalism, denying any disillusionment. They find themselves at spiritual crossroads, and must choose between emptiness and despair, and hope and peace in Christ.[24] Persons most apt to survive the disillusionment of young adulthood will learn patience and an openness to change. They will be disappointed, but will intentionally try to avoid bitterness, and move with patience to a clear understanding of life.

A unique feature of young adults in the 90's is that this disillusionment has not waited. It seems as if they have grown up disillusioned and wary. Society pressured them to grow up too fast. History swamped them almost before they got into the boat. The 1970's was, for folks born after 1961:

A nightmare of self-immersed parents, disintegrating homes, schools with conflicting missions, confused leaders, a culture shifting from G to R ratings, new public health dangers, and a "Me Decade" economy that tipped toward the organized old and away from the voiceless young. At every phase of life, 13ers have encountered a world of more punishing consequence than anything their elders ever knew.[25]

Young adults lack the quality role models necessary for successful living. Parents do not qualify. The government certainly does not qualify. Religion has generally failed to provide good models. Even their own "wannabe" music and film idols fall as their feet dissolve to muddy, drug-ridden sludge. They live in a confused society with no sense of center, no place to stand securely. No wonder one of the labels this current crop of young adults bears is the Disillusioned Generation![26]

The Results of Transitions
a) Flakiness

Like the comic strip character, Pigpen, who walks around in a perpetual cloud of dust, young adults seem to be walking in some kind of haze, or so older adults seem to think. It is easy to think that they are "flaky," inconsistent, capricious, indecisive. To label them "flaky" is not an inappropriate insult, nor is it to say anything that the more perceptive of them have not already recognized. One twenty-one year old put it this way:

What you need to understand is that we are "flakes." The biggest truth is that our word cannot be counted [on]. As long as our word cannot be believed or respected how are we going to have respect as a group. [27]

One reason for this reluctance to decide or commit is that growing up is unsettling. It is like riding one of those stomach-churning amusement park rides where you stand against the wall in a large cylinder in a circle. It starts to spin. As it gains speed it plasters you to the side while the floor drops away. You find yourself spinning at a hundred miles an hour with only centrifugal force keeping you from oblivion. When it is all over, you emerge exhilarated, relieved and terribly dizzy. Suddenly there is a sense of estrangement from all that has been familiar. The world has changed. All the rest of the day you have a vague feeling of having escaped some great, impending doom.

b) Estrangement

Estrangement is the result of deep personal and generational pain. Many experienced broken promises by parental or other authority for so long, that they see all authority with a jaundiced eye. They are cynical and mistrustful. Their life situations made them extremely self-reliant, and reluctant to trust others. They feel they can count on no one other than themselves. Their experience gives them no reason to trust, or commit to much of anything. If they do commit, they tend to wait for the last minute, or until they see value, benefits, or purpose in commitment. It is this tendency that their elders label as "flakiness." [28]

In their own way, and with differing intensities, all share this estrangement. Life is changing faster than they can cope. Transformations happen all the time. No wonder they seem preoccupied, and self-centered. The name of the young adult game is transition, change. It is a process much like that of a caterpillar becoming a butterfly. To understand their transitions, flakiness and estrangement is to understand them

Young adults see themselves at a threshold, ready to walk into a future filled with difficulties and possibilities. Yes, life-shaping transitions engulf them. Yes, they experience their generational uniqueness. Yes, they realize their sinfulness. In spite of all that, they still exude an innocence, an anticipation and a joy of life that is catching. This is what makes them so exciting to be around.

Intersection Number Five: *Culture*

Everyone at the winter retreat looked normal. The young women were casual in loose-fitting sweat shirts, warm pants and sports shoes. There was the normal mix of long and short hair. The young men dressed almost the same way: sweats, jeans, some shorts or T-shirts, even in winter, and sports shoes. There was the normal mix of long and short hair. The main difference was that the guys, almost to a man, were wearing some kind of duck-billed, baseball style cap, or "hat" as they call them.

Looking out over that mass of folks, it would be easy to assume that this was a homogeneous crowd. From a distance they all looked alike. They were there all together, participating as a temporary family of friends at worship and play.

A closer look, however, revealed the differences. Some were college students. Some were military. A few were Asian, Hispanic or African American. Others were from European backgrounds. Some, by birth or experience, were a mixture. A look at the registration revealed a United Nations of names. Yet, these young adults were all the same. They were Americans and, in this case, Christians. But the guys all wore their hats.

This small gathering of young adults is an example of the American cultural situation. While alike in many ways, all these folks together are different and unique. They are a cultural mosaic. They fit into a greater American framework as individual multi-hued, multi-textured pieces bound together by some element of common culture, and covered with a veneer of uniformity.[29] But all the guys all wore their hats.

Culture Defined

The dictionary defines human "culture" as "the concepts, habits, skills, arts, instruments, institutions, etc. of a given people in a given period; civilization."[30] These are the forces that impact how people, especially young adults, view themselves, relate to others and understand the world around them. Culture is taught, caught and learned. It is established by the birth or family context of the individual. It is taught by parents and teachers. People learn culture as they observe and participate in the life of their friends, family and the society around them. Young adults are products of culture at work on and within them simultaneously.[31]

Everyone knows you have to remove wrapper from the candy bar to eat it. Yet, it is the wrapper that defines it for the buying public. That is how you see it and buy it. That is what helps you tell a candy bar with chocolate and almonds from one with chocolate and a peanut butter filling. You discard the wrapper so you can savor the candy.

The cultural wrapper around young adults is just that, a wrapper, a facade. We need to understand that wrapping, that facade, that surrounds young adults, but also realize that the product inside is basically the same as when God created it so long ago. Young adults are like their predecessors in many ways. In many other ways, however, they are profoundly different. That is a difference produced by their culture, just like every other generation.

Factor: The Cultural Mosaic

Race is a reality. Skin color, eye shape, hair texture and color differentiate one group from another. Within the races body types differ, as do eye or hair color. While many commonalties exist among races, the human race varies infinitely. Like snowflakes, all humans are unique.

This generation was born into an American mix of cultures, languages and ethnic groups. As a group the generation born after 1965 is the most ethnically diverse in history. 70% of them are "white" or of "European" decent; 13% are African-American; 12% are Hispanic; 4% are Asian and 1% are Native American. [32] Because of this mix they are both aware of ethnic differences, and indifferent to them. They are open minded about racial mixing and interaction, and intolerant of intolerance. There is a widespread willingness to embrace racial and cultural differences, to denounce racism, and to be more open to immigrants than previous generations. Their spokesmen truthfully claim that ethnic and gender consciousness is reshaping society and setting important future trends. [33]

Result: Tension

Today's young adults experience new dimensions of cultural tension. They are like the casualties of the ancient torture in which the victim is tied with arms and legs attached to a different horse, each pulling toward opposing points on the compass. The cultures of their birth, their nation, their generation and contemporary society pull them in all directions at once.

Some are the children of recent immigrants, or recent immigrants themselves. Parents and heritage pull at them to follow ancient customs, retain their heart languages and gain education at all costs. A renewed cultural and even ethnic pride tugs at some.

Having experienced treatment as second-class citizens they now demand a share of America's wealth, but on their own terms. They will not tolerate prejudice or endure condescension. Some will flail against the system of society, breaking themselves upon it. Others will find ways to make the system work for them, wresting from it a place to stand.

Result: Mixing and Separation

Young adults mix more naturally than their predecessors with persons of other races and cultures. It is an almost universal experience to have friends of varied backgrounds, or neighbors of different races. Such friendships and interactions come because of the integrating of society. Economics or education have become the dividers of people that race was in the past. Education is open to all classes, languages and races. The mosaic is everywhere.

Yet, there is separation. The parts are distinguishable. Young adults collect together with their peers, who may be of the same race or language. Ethnic pride groups those who are the same. Young adults find themselves living in several worlds at the same time, and functioning equally well in all of them.

Factor: The New Culture Taking Shape

Beginning sometime during the decade of the sixties, something changed in North American culture. Radical advances in many areas of technology and knowledge changed the cultural playing field. In one of those rare, but totally transformational shifts, the whole world changed right under our noses.

Not only has the world changed, so have young adults. They are responding differently than their parents. Some writers have gone so far as to claim that there is a "radical generation gap" between this generation and their parents. This means that we must treat the new "Xer" generation differently than we treated the "Boomers." Xers react differently. This difference is not theoretical. It is real.[34] Kevin Graham Ford reports:

> *A profound shift in thinking has taken place in the space of a generation. Generation X is the first to see the world through post-modern eyes. My generation truly thinks differently, perceives differently, believes differently and processes truth differently than any previous generation.*[35]

That shift seemed to modify all the rules for living and existing. Suddenly living in the years after 1990, it seemed like a whole different planet. While a noted psychologist claimed that "men are from Mars, and women are from Venus,"[36] young adults often seem to their elders to be from Jupiter and beyond.[37]

It would take a thick book to describe this cultural change in depth. We can, however, identify several features of the social terrain that caused these changes.

Feature: The Media

About the time this generation was born, the visual media expanded dramatically. Broadcast television had to compete with cable and satellite service. The options multiplied from 3 or 4 channels to 50. Television became the omnipresent Cyclops babysitter for kids with keys to empty houses. Unsupervised, they watched and did whatever they wanted. The unblinking eye of TV became the mediator of the only morality they learned.[38]

Television is a way of life for young adults. They watch it on the average of three hours a day, and see as many as 90 movies a

year, broadcast, cable or taped. By the time they are twenty, they
have each spent close to 20,000 hours watching television. Without a doubt, they are the media people.[39]

Insightful observers claim the electronic media created contemporary youth culture by seeing an entire generation as one gigan-
tic market and acting to make it come true. These observers point
to MTV as the prime example of the media's impact on young
adults. The originators of MTV set out to become the creators of
a culture that wants what MTV, and any other merchandiser, sells.
The media creates a demand for products, and then fulfills that
demand. The media became the gatekeepers for young adult tastes
in clothing, language, leisure activities, technology, and sales of
tapes, videos and compact discs.[40]

This approach has been extremely successful. Young adults spend
millions of dollars on products they feel they "need" because television convinced them they did. This has happened because the
media have figured out that it is possible to combine entertainment and a sales pitch. Music videos featuring modern stars are
nothing more than exaggerated commercials. They urge viewers
to go out and purchase the recording, dress like the singer, and
buy into the values or lack of them the singer or the song promotes.[41]

The Result: Exploitation

Blatantly playing off a strong desire for relationship, the media
produce an artificial intimacy. Viewers feel connected with a larger
world because everyone wears the same kind of jeans, or sings
the same lyrics, or buys the same CD. Reality contorts as the
media attempt to trick them into perceiving rock performers and
TV personalities as more "real" than parents or friends. Because
this misdirection of relationships is often successful, the media

wield enormous influence. They shape the outward expressions of young adult life, those very things that tend to drive older adults crazy.[42]

Another result is the "entertain me" mindset. This is the feeling that you must always be doing "something," be seeing "something," or going "somewhere." It is a sense that nothing is happening unless you are receiving some kind of optical, aural, or sensual stimulation.

There is no mystery to this. After all, television, video games and other electronic gadgets were these folks' constant childhood companions. Those gizmos provided what they needed then. Why shouldn't they provide the same thing now? That is why video games, and the personal tape player are so popular. You can be alone with your closest friends, whom you've never met in person, as heard on their latest recording, "Thrash, Trash, and Smash It."[43]

The pervasive reality of this situation shows up in the instructions a youth minister gave his group as they prepared to go to a state-wide youth conference.

> *WHAT NOT TO BRING: Walkmans, Gameboys (a handheld video game), Any Electronic Device. If you bring one, Dave gets to keep it. We just want to get the most out of the conference. You can't build friendships with others and God with music blasting in your ears or your attention focused on a Gameboy. Remember why you are going on this trip!*

Constant media bombardment shuts out all other input. Young adults have little time for quiet consideration of their fast accumulating knowledge, or of the demands made on their emotions and wallets. Perhaps they are just as happy with it that way. When their minds are occupied, they don't have to remember their sorrow or pain, or the guilt from their bad choices. "Noise drives out unhappy thoughts, but is also smothers productive thought." Noise and the media are the opiate of these people. There is precious little quiet space for them to hear and heed the still small voice of God.[44]

Thirdly, media warp reality by minimizing and trivializing it. Sound bytes, visual fragments, and vanishing images portray life as discontinuous and fluid. Television telescopes time, crunching days and hours into minutes. Everything is temporary and discardable. "The single, individual identity disappears in a swirling montage of discontinuous fragments." True wholeness becomes the goal of a generation fragmented by its entertainment. Real community must break through the opiate of a false community based solely on the shared viewing of a sparkling package of pixels.[45]

Familiarity has, however, bred a wide-spread "savvyness" about the media. Young adults can differentiate between the real and the unreal, between virtual violence and real violence. Thousands of TV viewing hours have gave them a sensitivity to information and manipulation. They know from experience that TV distorts the truth, and is, as often as not, one long commercial hawking soap, soda, sex and action figures. It is no longer their one-eyed god, dictating every thought. It is more a window to the world, an access point to communities, far and near. It is a companion, with whom they have an almost organic relationship, a tool for knowledge and entertainment, a way to spend time relaxing.

Sometimes television is totally engrossing; sometimes it is wallpaper. It often reflects values, lives, and interests different from their own. For years it echoed only the speech patterns of their elders. Television often amuses. It frequently lies.[46]

Feature: The Economy

Folk born after 1961 enter adulthood with an automatic economic conflict. They grew up either with many possessions provided by their parents or with the knowledge that such possessions were possibilities. Many are consummate consumers. They have discretionary wealth of about $35 a week gladly provided by workaholic parents who confuse economic success with personal happiness.[47] This pattern begins in the teen years and continues into young adulthood. They consider it an immutable right to have "stuff" and gadgets.[48] They want the latest and the newest, and think nothing of dropping $50 or $60 for a pair of pants or two or three music CDs. They do not blink when asked to pay $30 for a cotton T-shirt with a silk-screened brand name logo.

Adulthood, however, thrusts them into a revised economic situation. Decisions their parents made to save money have hurt them. The prime example is California's tax reform measure, Proposition 13. The result of a tax-payer revolt against escalating property taxes, Proposition 13 was a voted into law by Boomer parents in the late '70's. This was good for property owners, but bad for public education. Income for education from property taxes all but ceased, but cost increases continued. The end result of all of that was a loss of quality and services in education. The so-called educational frills like art, music, shop, extracurricular sports, became optional and at extra cost. The children of the Boomers suffered from their parents' misplaced financial conservatism. Parents had to pay after all, as schools required students to purchase supplies, rent instruments and pay fees for sports and band trips, practices unheard of in the middle decades of this century.[49]

During the last three decades of this century we saw stable infla-
tion, but soaring costs. Everything, clothes, houses, education to
name a few, costs more, while buying power is stagnant or dry-
ing up. The financial rewards of working such as salaries and
benefits have fallen behind.[50] Job markets no longer belong to
the seller. Employed high school graduates earn 27% less today
and similar grads did in 1979.[51] Corporations no longer regularly
provide automatic five figure salaries for promising college graduates. The "American dream" seems beyond their grasp. [52]

The Result: Economic Ambivalence

Young adults put career in its proper place as a means to a greater
end. That end may be wholeness, acceptance, or some other deeper
aspect of life. This attitude will open doors for ministry, and service for believers. It will also set the stage for another cultural
change, as they will instill a more "civic" approach to life in their
children.[53]

Negatively for the current generation, the possession habit is difficult to break. For many, the drive to possess, and its increasing
difficulty shapes their values. This shows itself in the loss of a
"job for job's sake" work ethic. They reject any baby boomer style
approach to success. A job is a means to the end of obtaining
possessions and the resources to enjoy their free time. For some
it is a means of basic survival. Career is not necessarily an end in
itself as with their predecessors.[54]

The harsh reality for almost 50% of young adults is that the hope
for substantial financial stability does not exist at all. Whole seg-
ments of this group face adulthood with no likelihood of moving
beyond entry level minimum wage jobs. A recent study of the
"forgotten half" of the young adult population points that may of
them will start their adult lives in an "economic limbo of unem-
ployment, part-time jobs, and poverty wages. Many of them never

break free." Our society seems to be having difficulty ensuring all our young adults the opportunity to face the future with a sense of economic confidence and security. Whether we accept the fact or not, young adults are in danger of becoming an economically deprived, severely unhappy social under-class.[55]

Feature: Relative Truth

Reflecting our prevailing culture, most young adults are suspicious of or openly reject the idea of absolute truth. They do not see truth as final or based on actuality. Truth, rather, is relative, based on my experience or your experience. Therefore, everything is relative and everything is true. This is reality perceived in subjective, not objective terms. What is true for you, just might not be true for me. Not only do many of them not believe in absolute truth, they also are not so sure that anyone can actually know what truth is. [56]

Ethics and morality have also taken a hit in this relativistic age. It is very much like the era of the Old Testament Judges when "everyman did what was right in his own eyes." *(Judges 17:6)* Young adults have accepted the cultural pattern that places the individual squarely in the center of the universe, and which makes personal well being and existence the focus and determinant of life. This idolatrous humanism has redirected the focus of morality and truth from God to the individual. Josh McDowell describes the moral situation:

> *I believe that one of the prime reasons this generation is setting new records for dishonesty, disrespect, sexual promiscuity, violence, suicide, and other pathologies, is because they have lost their moral underpinnings; their foundational belief in morality and truth has been eroded.*[57]

Result: A Generation With No Solid Place to Stand

Belief leads to behavior. Belief in relative truth with no objective foundation apart from the individual leads to an idolatry of the self. People are no longer treated as worthy and valuable. They are seen only as means to an end of self-gratification.

Young adults believing in relative truth have no moral anchor for their lives. They are adrift in a sea of whim, and fancy. They are at the mercy of whatever "truth" or "morality" that makes the most noise and offers the most reward for the moment. As a result, immoral behavior becomes the norm. People have value only as objects of someone else's gratification. Abuse and immoral behavior abound. George Barna describes their condition:

> *They have not had the requisite time to explore the mysteries and snares of the world without external expectations. They have not had the opportunity to plumb the depths of their characters, to figure out who they really are or to learn more about what is really important to them. They have been robbed of the incubation period necessary to allow their minds, bodies and spirits to develop more fully and get in synch before dealing with the enormously complex realities of life in a "civilized" society at the close of the twentieth century.*[58]

The extent of contemporary moral relativity emerges in surveys conducted by Josh McDowell and the Barna Research Group. In 1994 they polled 3,700 Christian youth from all denominations on a variety of moral issues. The survey demonstrated that even church-going youths are having difficulty knowing and doing what is moral and ethical. The surveys disclosed them to be "living on the moral edge, closer to disaster than we ever imagined."[59] It is hard to know which is more distressing, that Christian young adults are, for example, more promiscuous than they used to be, or that their guilt about doing these things is so low. This situation places fallen society where it has always been, as an adversary to the Gospel. In response the Church offers that Gospel as a viable remedy to the emptiness of moral relativity, and as that anchor on which young adults may tie their lives.

Feature: Family Disruption

For whatever reasons, the family at the end of the twentieth century is in transition, some would say trouble. The census indicates tremendous rises in the divorce rate, the percentage of single parent households, and the number of biological, but unmarried parents. This situation impacts young adults because they are the children of divorce and single parenting. Nearly 50% come from broken homes. They were latchkey kids during their elementary years, who had television for a baby sitter. They experienced neglect or indulgence, sometimes with nothing in between.[60]

The Result: Emotional Calluses

Three young adult character traits relate directly to their experience of family disruption. These become calluses on their souls.

They know brokenness, pain and helplessness. If their parents divorced, they felt responsible. If there was verbal abuse they huddled in fear. If there was physical abuse they cringed in terror, thirsting for revenge. Their own anger rose and ate away at them as they helplessly endured the abuse. If they were latch-key kids they felt the loneliness of an empty house, and the lack of guidance during their free time. Childhood, usually reserved for these kinds of things, gave them no sense of security and family. As adults they must now seek these thing in places other than at home and from people other than their biological family.[61]

They have small respect for authority. Broken families blurred their understanding and experience of adult authority. Those in charge often seem at odds with one another. While the custodial parent did not allow a behavior or activity, the weekend dad, or mom, did. Confusion resulted, especially when they were young. Because parental authority was uncertain, disrespect for all authority resulted.

They are cynical and suspicious. Who would not be, if they survived a childhood of postponed or broken parental promises? Who would not be, if their hopes and dreams were repeatedly built up only to be dashed to pieces by parental irresponsibility? When those who are responsible for loving and supporting you do not, you have no recourse but cynicism and suspicion.

They can deal with complexity. When broken families happen, new family configurations result. Not only do you have a mom and a dad, you have stepmoms and stepdads, and live-in "uncles," and perhaps ex-stepmoms and stepdads. Step-siblings, grandparents, aunts, uncles, and cousins seem to multiply like rabbits. While the nuclear family is disrupted, the extended family is expanding. In a positive situation this could be a large web of people to care for and love you. Negatively, it could mean that you need a score card to keep everyone straight.

Feature: Abortion

Baby Busters are victims of an unprecedented moral crisis. Nationally, they number 79 million after abortion. If there had been no or few abortions, the generation could number over 100 million persons. This would have been no baby bust, and the entire cultural picture for this generation would have been different.[62]

Result: A Generation of Victims

Parental attitudes about abortion and divorce gave rise to a "throw away" mentality. Commitment became unnecessary, even dangerous. Relationships were intentionally temporary and disposable. Young adults only have their parents' bad examples to follow. If their relationships went bad, they disposed of the problem person. If they had unwanted pregnancy, abortion was readily available. Life was cheapened. Rather than feeling wanted because they survived the abortion holocaust, young adults suspect they are next.

Feature: AIDS

The new, unwanted outcome of recreational sex is no longer just an unwanted pregnancy, or inconvenient, but treatable venereal disease. It is AIDS, acquired immune deficiency syndrome, the black plague of our day. No longer confined to an aberrant segment of society, this highly contagious virus is spreading throughout the general population.[63]

Result: Sexual Roulette

Now days Russian roulette is no longer played with a pistol. Young adults regularly play it with each other's bodies when they engage in casual, recreational sex. It is a deadly game they face with either a studied nonchalance, or a stolid fatalism.

Society may preach loud and long about protected sex. The church may proclaim the Biblical high ground of sexual chastity. Some will heed these words, while others will just take their chances. For the general young adult population, however, there is no stopping sexual expression. Until science finds a true cure, AIDS will continue to spread among the sexually active. Young adults will have to factor this danger into their lives. They will experience the loss of friends or their own health to this disease. They will be forced to deal with its society-wide consequences.

Intersection Number Six:
Desire

In the movie, <u>Indiana Jones and the Last Crusade</u> the hero quests for the elusive Holy Grail, the cup used by Jesus at the Last Supper. Finally, he approaches the cave where the Grail is resting. He comes through a passage in the cavern wall opening to a seemingly bottomless chasm. There he stands, teetering on the brink of disaster. The Holy Grail's resting place is within sight, but just out of grasp. His choices are few. He cannot retreat, and advance seems like sure death. He must decide. Does he have the faith to follow the promise of the ancient clues, or will he die right there? Will he act or be paralyzed? After an agonizing moment he makes his choice. Slowly, cautiously, he steps out into the empty void. Then, he is surprised and gratified to discover a solid walkway that allows him to cross safely. Practically for him, faith made a way.

Young adults desire growth, but are teetering on the brink. They need assurance that when they step out there will be something solid on which to stand. This is where the church can find its point of contact. It is at this point of desire that Christ can intersect their lives.

Surveys and conversations with over three hundred young adults have shown specific things they want from the church. The manner and intensity with which they receive these things will directly impact their response to the church. For a church to have any real influence in their lives, it must speak to these desires just to get a hearing.

Desire # 1: They want understanding and respect.
Everyone wants someone else to understand them, but young adults want it more. Our society gives mixed signals about them.

It cannot decide if they are spoiled children, to humor, or punish, or if they are truly adults worthy of recognition as productive members. We have no ritual, rite or celebration marking the transition from childhood to adulthood. It is just one long gray period, with a definite beginning (high school graduation) but no precise ending. No wonder they are confused.

Everyone wants respect, but young adults want it more. They need regular reassurance that they have respect. Older folks need to affirm this again and again. The young man did not mince his words as he described his feelings about respect:

> *You can't expect people our age to try to keep up a relationship with adults if they are not going to respect us; if they are constantly looking down on us. Just listen to us. We are not stupid. We know what we are doing most of the time. Even if we are wrong, still listen to us. There may be something there. Don't blow us off. We are not little kids.* [64]

A perceived lack of "respect" causes a loss of credibility, a breach of relationship, which is slow to mend. Close friendships can become distant ones if there is disrespect.

The question is then, "What is there for others to respect?"

First, respect young adults because Christ respected them first. Respect for young adults springs from the fact that Christ died for them, too. It is scriptural to respect them. They are part of the "whosoever" of John 3:16. That truth is a solid foundation for the respect they want and deserve.

Second, respect them for their potential. Each young adult is a grand bundle of potentialities for love, service, enthusiasm, growth and ministry. Remember, events that took place during their young adult years shaped the lives of many Christian leaders. Remember, it was as young adults that most missionaries made their first-time decision to serve God in a foreign land, or recommitted to an earlier decision.

<u>Third, respect them for their talents and abilities</u>. It is our insecurities that blind us to the talents young adults have to rival or surpass our own. They are often very skilled in a chosen field, task or profession. Their years of schooling and training are beginning to pay off. They have gained proficiency in a number of areas, and can do a great deal more than we might think they can. Give them a chance!

<u>Fourth, respect them for their optimism, enthusiasm, and energy</u>. Young adults are beginning to taste the difficulties of life. They are not naive about the dangers of adulthood. Society, the media, government and social trends have seen to that. Yet, in spite of their cynicism, they are eager to have their own chance at life. Their energy is ready and available. Their commitment to a cause is genuine, if often tentative. Yet, the church can harness that optimism, enthusiasm and energy for Christ's sake.

It is difficult for those hardened by life's adversities to consider those whom they perceive as having not "paid their dues." It is difficult to appreciate those who seem cocky and self-assured or arrogant or just plain naive. Yet that is the paradox of ministry. To reach this group for Christ, we must respect those we think do not deserve it. Is not that what Jesus meant when he said, "For whosoever wishes to save his life shall lose it; but whoever loses his life for My sake and the gospel's shall save it?" *(Mark 9:35)*

Desire # 2: They want connection.

Young adults want to belong, first to each other, and then to a broader, adult family. They want to belong as adults, and sit at the main table at Thanksgiving. They do not want adults to consider them babies, left to sit with the real children at the game table in the other room. Theirs is a search for a connected, integrated life that is local and within their reach.[65]

Acceptance and Family

The "family" they need is more extended than nuclear. It must encompass more people than parents or siblings. They are pulling away from parents, but not for the need for family. They will find acceptance. They will find family and connection.

This desire is a great opportunity for the church. We can provide the welcoming environment that makes connection possible. We can become a second family at the time when their relation with their first family is tense. For some, we can provide a positive alternative to a negative home life.

There are at least two ways the church can do this. The first is to be the catalyst for them to connect with each other. Provide the opportunities and the environment, and the connection will happen by itself.

The second way for family to happen is with the entire church. The church must communicate a sense of welcome and family, for everyone, not just the "in" crowd, or the older folks. In the case of young adults, the church must go out of its way to welcome them in and make them feel included. It is not enough for the church to assume that is happening. This means that we must take young adults seriously.

We must intentionally involve them in the life, ministry and leadership of the church. Involvement in the total church family begins with invitations to lunch, continues with relationships, responsibilities and strong reminders, and culminates with participation in the church's power structures. Family starts with an attitude of welcome, and acceptance. When it happens, it draws young adults to it like iron to a magnet.

Intimacy
According to psychologist Erick Erickson the search for intimacy is a major young adult task. He defines it as the "capacity to commit oneself to concrete affiliations that may call for significant sacrifices and compromises." [66] Intimacy is a relationship that allows for the one person to share the deepest personal issues with another person without fear of ridicule or rejection. When intimacy happens, all facades disappear.

In order for intimacy to be possible, young adults must first overcome the "Ninja Turtle" syndrome. The "Ninja Turtle" syndrome is the feeling of having been discarded as a child. (The turtles were flushed into the sewers as babies.) It is a dream world of being able to hide in some dank retreat with their friends and eat pizza. It is the fantasy of emerging into the real world as super heroes to fight Evil and defend some beautiful girl, or guy. There is safety in this. If things get too tough, if people get too "close," they can always retreat into their insulated shells, or underground hideaways.[67]

Yet they crave closeness. They desire to open themselves in relationships. They want real friendship and the freedom to share their deepest feelings. They want sex to be more than recreation and exercise. They want it to be an expression of real love. Most of all, they want to communicate and to commit. It is one of the most difficult things they are trying to do.

Desire #3: They want the unvarnished truth.

Nothing so appeals to young adults as the "unvarnished truth." They reject superficial, "nice" Bible stories. They want the reality behind those stories. It is not enough to know *that* Delilah cut Samson's hair, or that Jesus fed the five thousand, or that Moses led the Israelites out of Egypt. They must know *why* it happened, and how it impacts their lives right now. A sugar-coated gospel is not for them. Life has hit them hard enough, even by age 18, that they know they need a strong, prophetic, adult word from the Lord. They need it to survive life, and to become the productive leaders they feel they should, ought and are called by God to be.

In a discussion group one young adult reacted to the statement that his generation wanted the "unvarnished truth." He said,

> *I would personally underline, circle, draw arrows to this. I would personally interpret "telling the unvarnished truth" as stripping off the sugar coating and telling the truth, and not just making this [a] happy story that happened 2,000 years ago. Let's tell the truth. Let's get down, and if it hurts, its supposed to.*[68]

On the value of the truth, another young man in the same discussion group spoke of coming to know real truth in the person of Jesus Christ. He said,

> *It wakes you up faster than you can even imagine. He [God] is awesome, but sometimes like you love your father; but your father is the one who spanks you when you get in trouble. I know that woke me up to a lot of things I need to learn.*[69]

While they desire heavy doses of reality, they demand that the truth be told in love, without condescension or prejudice. Anyone who tells them the truth must do so after first respecting and being respected, accepting and being accepted by them. They are willing to take the bitter pill of starkly real truth, whether from Scripture, or from life, but would rather have it from allies and friends than adversaries.

Desire # 4: They crave responsibility and accountability.

One of God's strongest natural laws seems to be that maturity and strength comes only through struggle. Assist a butterfly to emerge by cutting the cocoon and you end up with a dull, weak, deformed creature unable to soar and feed. Leave it alone in its struggle of emergence and you will soon discover a beautiful, multicolored creature capable of flying thousands of miles.

The cry of young adults is for a tension in their emerging adulthood. They want to struggle, to strain against the restraints, and to emerge strong, capable, trained and ready to move on. They want responsibility thrust upon them. This must come either as a sign of respect, or a challenge to "put up or shut up." They know they are capable of carrying out many of the responsibilities of adulthood, and are willing to take them on.

By responsibilities we mean the leadership roles, the "power" and influence that can come to "elders" in the church. Young adults want in on the decision making processes. They want their opinions to count and to be implemented by the church at large. They are willing to become involved in all aspects of church life.

Accountability is a great motivator. Since they recognize that they are novices, and apprentices, they are willing to submit to appropriate accountability. It holds them to their own standards. For them it is a recognition of full acceptance into the rigors of adult leadership.

Having the "power," and being called to account for it does say that they have in some part "arrived" at full adulthood. It also places them in a real and often uncomfortable internal tension. Are they children or adults? The tensions do lead to ambiguities and inconsistencies of action. They do sometimes seem like "flakes" at times, and often do "flake" off into irresponsibility. Leaders of young adults must be strong enough to hold them to this tension, and must thrive in it. For it is only as young adults are held in the tensions imposed by responsibility and account-ability that they emerge as full-grown adults.

Desire #5: They want mentors.

Young adults want guidance in this business of being "adult." They need instruction. One of them put it this way:

> *I think the only older Christians that [young adults] really get to deal with are their parents, and that is not always the best way to hear information and get guid-ance. If more churches were to promote mentoring relationships with people of the same sex, but 10-20 years older that them, it would really help.*[70]

Relationships with older adults are important to these folks. They want a "non-threatening authority figure" in their lives. Often the cannot have this kind of relationship with their parents. Pride, the wounds left over from parental failure and the remnants of adolescent rebellion make this difficult. They are willing and de-sirous, however, of accepting direction from some other older adult who comes to them with no prior emotional baggage. This is an adult with whom they can have a relationship based totally on their own identity, and from whom they can learn and grow.

Mentoring has to do with skill development and character. Mentors can teach the "inside" information about certain areas, as well as the basics. They can also teach something far more valuable: character and spiritual maturity. They can be sounding boards, and advice givers, building on relationships of mutual respect and understanding.

Desire #6: They desire spirituality and God.

Among Non-Believers

We understand the general population to be vaguely spiritual. Like Paul's listeners at Mars Hill, they "are very religious in all respects" *(Acts 17:22)*. Their spirituality is unfocused, but intense.

> *They are, after all, the first generation of Americans to be raised without the culturally established assumption that they would start their religious explorations with Christianity and continue to seek a faith system only if Christianity was found wanting. The belief system maintained by most is a combination of Christianity, pragmatism, Far Eastern traditions and utilitarianism. They are not opposed to Christianity. They simply see no compelling reason to choose one faith over another if they don't have to.*[71]

Among Believers

The God of Scripture draws young adults to Himself. They can see that knowing God and interacting with him can give them the "swift kick" they know they need:

> *God is an awesome God. He is ever caring and loving and He has done the most wonderful things. At the same time the Bible says to fear Him. That is when I*

learned the most and actually applied what I had learned to my life. It is awesome when you learn how to fear God. It wakes you up faster than you can even imagine. He is awesome, but sometimes He is like your father who spanks you when you get in trouble. I see sometimes that we don't learn. Jesus Christ will pun-ish you when you do wrong. I know that woke me up to a lot of things I need to learn. [72]

Conclusion

Young have their shopping list of desires. Just ask them. They want among a lot of other things respect and understanding, con-nection, the truth, responsibility and accountability, mentors and most importantly they want God. They want those intangibles which amplify their humanity and honor their adulthood. As the church seeks to intersect their lives, it must do so at the point of their desires, and in so doing remembering the words of Proverbs 13:12: "Hope deferred makes the heart sick, but desire fulfilled is a tree of life."

Intersection Number Seven:
Dynamic Energy

It does not take long to discover that young adults have energy to spare. Just walk into any large gathering of this group, especially religious ones. There is an electricity in the air. Call it enthusiasm. Call it raging hormones. It is there, a palpable presence. Observe how they greet each other, like long lost soul mates, rushing to greet their friends with cries and even squeals of joy. Bone crushing hugs and hearty back thumping are common sights. Even the most re-served greet each other with elaborate handshakes, and almost ritual decorum.

They are Dynamic in Leadership.

Watch young adults interacting with one another for clues to their powerful potential. They move and talk with excitement. They are electric. No wonder they react negatively to hints of petrified orthodoxy. A petrified tree only looks like a tree. It is as lifeless as the rock it is. Young adults want life and energy, not a dead formality.

Young adults are at their physical and mental peak. Vibrant and excited, every facility they have is poised for action. They have no dulled perceptions. They are ready to spread their wings and try out what they have learned. [73]

As a group they are a dynamic force, with energy, time, enthusiasm. Its members have not had their visionary idealism tainted by the cares and harsh realities of the world. While still disillusioned, they have not lost their will to advance. These characteristics place them in the unique position of being able to launch movements, start trends, and influence civilizations. This is especially true in the life of the Christian faith.

Scripture Reminds Us They are Dynamic Leaders.

Scripture itself is full of young adults at the forefront of national and spiritual leadership. David was winning his reputation as a freedom fighter as a young adult *(1 Samuel 18-31)*. A youthful Paul was zealously persecuting the Christians when he encountered the Risen Christ *(Acts 8:1-5, 9:1-31)*. Timothy's mentor, Paul, encouraged him to "let no one look down on your youthfulness" *(1 Timothy 4: 12)* while he was fresh into his first pastorate. Most importantly, Jesus himself was barely into his thirties when he began to preach the good news to Israel *(Luke 3:23, Mark 1: 15)*.

Christian History Proves They Are Dynamic Leaders.

A quick review of history plainly shows this age-group's dynamic leadership. It is not surprising, that most of the great molders of that history were young adults. They easily become dissatisfied with the religious tradition of their birth. Something about their youthful energy, idealism, and search for truth motivates them to seek and establish a purer religious ideal.[74]

Luther

Martin Luther was 30 when he sought a more Biblical faith. He studied scripture, especially the book of Romans. There he realized that the religion of the day had crippled God's grace with hobbles of legalism. Proclaiming, "By grace are ye saved through faith, not of works," *(Ephesians 2:8-9)* he challenged the Roman Catholic establishment in Wittenberg, and set in motion the Protestant Reformation.

The Anabaptists

The scriptural doctrine of believers' baptism had no place in the doctrine of the established churches. Three young adult seminary students in Zurich rediscovered it through a correct reading of the Greek New Testament. Felix Manz, 27 and Conrad Grebel, 28, along with several others, received believers' baptism on a cold January day in 1525. Within four years all had met martyrs' deaths. Their brave commitment led to a powerful new religious movement that spread across Europe. It gave birth to the so-called "Radical Reformation," and counts modern day Baptists among its spiritual progeny.

John Calvin

John Calvin was 26 when he published his master work, *The Institutes of the Christian Religion,* in 1536. This was a deep theological treatise written to defend French and Swiss Protestants. It still is the foundation document for an entire wing of the Protestant Reformation. The Presbyterian and Reformed denominations owe their existence to this young adult.[75]

Modern Foreign Missions

Caught out in the rain in the summer of 1806, several Christian college students found shelter under a nearby haystack. A prayer meeting ensued. The outcome of this now famous "Haystack Prayer Meeting" was that all dedicated their lives to foreign mission service. Two of those, Adoniram Judson and Luther Rice, later became Baptists, and helped mobilize that denomination, both northern and southern branches, for world-wide missions. Church historians point to that event as the beginning of the modern foreign missions movement among American evangelicals. Young adults made it happen.[76]

Young adults continue to spark the missions and volunteer movements of churches across the country. The Student Volunteer Movement in the 20's, with John R. Mott, 25, as its leader, declared its goal to be "To win the world for Christ in our lifetime."[77] Southern Baptists aided that goal during the thirty year period from 1965 to 1995 by sending 2,650 young adults overseas for missionary service. [78] Those young adults served with the same grand goal in mind.

Contemporary Society Confirms Their Dynamic Leadership.

As this generation has matured, the common wisdom that says they are nothing but slackers has proven to be false. Nothing can be farther from the truth. The majority of young adults today want to succeed and advance in life. They are not a lost generation, invisible to the general public. They are very evident in the real world.

An article, "Generalizations X," in the June 6, 1994, issue of *Newsweek* debunks any allegations of laziness on the part of this generation. It lists 35 people in their twenties who can in no way be labeled slackers. The list includes artists, entrepreneurs, mayors, actors, magazine editors, professional athletes, political professionals and entertainers. [79]

More recently, *Time* reports, "Slackers? Hardly. The so-called Generation X turns out to be full of go-getters who are just doing it but their way." It goes on to say that a recent survey showed today's young adults have unprecedented purchasing power, a sense of destiny, and a strong desire to compete. They are entrepeneuers and risk takers. For many the watchword is, "My generation believes we can do almost anything." Not only a watchword, it is being realized daily.[80]

Look around with eyes open to this age group and be surprised. You will discover "buster" young adults coaching your son's basketball team, pastoring your church, and leading the missions outreach of local groups of churches. The idea that this generation is any less intense and ambitious than its predecessors is just a myth.

Today's young adults are living out their potential. They are exerting leadership in all areas of life. It is true that not all young adults are leaders. It is also true that some are at the front of the pack, people not afraid to take risks, work and lead.

Conclusion

As the Gospel of Jesus intersects and transforms lives, the road they travel is altered. Young adults can find a new highway to travel, highway that, though narrow offers the most direct route to their hearts' desires. Individual believers, those called to minister to young adults, can be the ones to help it all happen.

[1] William Mahedy and Janet Bernardi, A Generation Alone, (Downers Grove, Ill.: InterVarsity Press, 1994), 24.

[2] Romans 1:18-2:16.

[3] John Verteufeuill, "Lowering the Odds of Sexual Promiscuity," Youthworker, Summer, 1989, 36. George Barna. The Invisible Generation: Baby Busters, (Glendale, Ca.: Barna Research, 1992), 144-145.

[4] Josh McDowell and Bob Hostetler, Right from Wrong, (Dallas, Tx.: Word Publishing, 1994), 268-269. Mahedy and Bernardi, A Generation Alone, 95.

[5] Mahedy and Bernardi, A Generation Alone, 95, 101. Kevin Graham Ford, Jesus for a New Generation, (Downers Grove, Ill.: InterVarsity Press, 1995), 92.

[6] Kevin Ford, Jesus for a New Generation, 92-93.

[7] Erik Frederick Harteis, "Theme for Generation X," Sojourners, November, 1994, 19.

[8] Donald Joy, "Religious, Moral, and Faith Development in Young Adults," in Handbook of Young Adult Religious Education. (Birmingham, Ala. (Religious Education Press, 1995, edited by Harley Atkinson), p. 141. George Barna, Generation Next: What You Need To Know About Today's Youth. (Ventura, Ca.: Regal Books, 1995), 10, 20.

[9] Barna, Generation Next, 74.See George Gallup, Jr. And Robert Bezilla, The Religious life of Young Americans (Princeton, N.J.: The George II. Gallup International Institute, 1992), 12-14, 17, and Barna, Generation Next, 73-83.

[10] Douglas Coupland, Life After God (New York: Pocket Books, 1994), 273f., 359.

[11] Mahedy and Bernardi A Generation Alone, 48. Ford, Jesus for a New Generation, 94. Jeffrey R. Bantz, Generation X (Miami: Latin American Mission, 1995), 89.

[12] Clifford T. Gribbon, Developing Faith in Young Adults: Effective Ministry with 18-35 Year Olds (New York: The Alban Institute, 1990), 16.

[13] Gribbon, Dev. Faith, 39.

[14] Gribbon, Dev. Faith, 20.

[15] Gribbon, Dev. Faith, 25.

[16] Arthur Chickering, Education and Identity, (San Francisco, Ca: Jossey-Bass, Inc. Publishers, 1969), 23.

[17] "Baby Busters" are marrying later than their Baby Boomer counterparts. In 1970 only 19% of the 25-29 year old males had never married, and 11% of women in the same age group. By 1993 that number had risen to 48% of man and 33% of women 25-29 years of age. Parade Magazine, September 10, 1995, 28.

[18] Erik Erikson, Childhood and Society. Second Edition, (New York: W.W. Norton & Company, Inc., 1963), 261-263.

[19] Gribbon, Dev. Faith, 20.

[20] Les Steele. "Psychological Characteristics of Young Adults," in Atkinson, ed. Handbook, 97.

[21] Gribbon, Dev. Faith, 39.

[22] Gribbon, Dev. Faith, 23.

[23] Gribbon, Dev. Faith. 25.

[24] Mahedy and Bernardi, A Generation Alone, 69.

[25] William Strauss and Neil Howe, Generations: A History of America's Future, 1584-2069 (New York: William Morrow, 1991), 321.

[26] Dieter Zander, "The Gospel for Generation X", Leadership, Spring, 1995, p. 37. Strauss and Howe, Generations, 322.

[27] Jenness Park Focus Group, July, 1995.

[28] Bruce Tulgan, Managing Generation X (Santa Monica, Ca.: Merritt Publishing, 1995), 8-9. Ford, Jesus for a New Generation, 147. Tim Celek and Deiter Zander, Inside the Soul of a New Generation (Grand Rapids: Zondervan Publishing House, 1996), 15, 25. Mahedy and Bernardi, A Generation Alone, 32. 47.

[29] Oscar Romo, American Mosaic: Church Planting in Ethnic America (Nashville, Tn.: Broadman Press, 1993), 17, 41.

[30] "Culture," Webster's New World Dictionary of the American Language (New York: The World Publishing Company, 1956), 358.

[31] Ruth Benedict, Patterns of Culture (New York: Mentor Books, 1934), 25-28.

[32] Jeff Giles, "Generalizations X," Newsweek, June 6, 1994, 66

[33] Ford, Jesus for a New Generation, 84.

[34] Karen Ritchie, Marketing to Generation X (New York: Lexington Books, 1995), 14; Bruce Tulgan, Managing Generation X, (Santa Monica, Ca.: Merrit Publishing, 1995), 21.

[35] Ford, Jesus for a New Generation, 113.

[36] John Gray, Men are From Mars, Women Are From Venus (New York: Harper Collins Publishers , 1992).

[37] Robert Ludwig. "Twentysomethings: Struggling to Find a Meaningful Life," The Catholic World. September/October, 1995. Vol. 238:1427, 197.

[38] Kevin Graham Ford, "My So-Called Generation: A Buster Speaks." The Ivy Jungle Report, Vol. 4, Fall, 1995, 8.

[39] Ford, "My So-Called Generation," 8. Dieter Zander, "Baby Busters: How to Reach A New Generation," Fuller Evangelistic Association, 1992.

[40] Quentin K. Schultze, et al., Dancing In the Dark (Grand Rapids, Mi.: Eerdmans, 1991), 51.

[41] Schultze, et al., Dancing in the Dark, 132.

[42] Raines and Bradford, TwentySomething, 14.

[43] Ford, Jesus for a New Generation, 55.

[44] Alan J. Roxburg, Reaching a New Generation: Strategies for Tomorrow's Church, (Downers Grove,Ill.: InterVarsity Press, 1993), 38-40.

[45] Celek and Zander, Inside the Soul of the New Generation, 62-65. Karen Ritchie, Marketing to Generation X, (New York: Lexington Books, 1995), 122.

[46] Ritchie, Marketing to Generation X, 63.

[47] Gary McIntosh, "The McIntosh Church Growth Network", August, 1990, Volume Two, Number Eight.

[48] Strauss and Howe, Generations, 325.

[49] Strauss and Howe, Generations, 320.

[50] Kent Jones, "The Spin: talkin' 'bout our generation," Seventeen, August, 1993, 131.

[51] Strauss and Howe, Generations, 335-341.

[52] Dieter Zander, "The Gospel for Generation X", Leadership, Spring 1995, Volume XVI, Number 2, 37.

[53] Straus and Howe, Generations, p. 335f.

[54] Zander, "Gospel for Generation X", p. 27.

[55] "The Forgotten Half: Pathways to Success for America's Youth and Young Families," Washington D.C.: The William T. Grant Foundation Commission on Work, Family, and Citizenship, 1988, 1.

[56] Zander, "The Gospel for Generation X," 18. Barna, Generation Next, 32-33. Josh McDowell and Bob Hostetler, Right From Wrong (Dallas, Tx.: Word Publishihng, 1994), 3-16. Ford, Jesus for a New Generation, 125-129.

[57] McDowell, Right From Wrong, 12.

[58] Barna, Generation Next, 42.

[59] McDowell, Right From Wrong, 8.

[60] Strauss and Howe, Generations, 324. Zander, "The Gospel for Generation X," 37.

[61] Celek and Zander, Inside the Soul of a New Generation, pp. 16, 25,36, 54. Ford. Jesus for a New Generation, 47. Mahedy and Bernardi, A Generation Alone, 24.

[62] Strauss and Howe, Generations, 318, 324.

[63] William M. Tillman, Jr. AIDS: A Christian Response. (Nashville, Tn.: Convention Press, 1990), 11-12.

[64] Jenness Park Focus Group, July 1995.

[65] Roxburgh, Reaching a New Generation, 23.

[66] Quoted in Les Steele, "Psychological Characteristics of Young Adults," in Atkinson, ed., Handbook, 99.

[67] Strauss and Howe, Generations, 323.

[68] Jenness Park Focus Group, July 1995.

[69] Jenness Park Focus Group, July 1995.

[70] Jenness Park Focus Group, July 1995.

[71] George Barna, Generation Next, 74.

[72] Jenness Park Focus Group, July 1995.

[73] John Elias, "Purpose and Scope of Young Adult Religious Education" in Atkinson, ed., Handbook, 34.

[74] John Elias, "Purpose and Scope of Young Adult Religious Education" in Atkinson, ed. Handbook, 12.

[75] Williston Walker, et al. A History of the Christian Church. Fourth Edition (New York: Charles Scribner's Sons, 1985), Luther: 422-426; Anabaptists: 448; Jean Calvin: 473.

[76] Sidney E. Ahlstrom, A Religious History of the American People (New Haven: Yale University Press. 1972) , 423-424.

[77] Ahlstrom, A Religious History, 865-6.

[78] "Foreign Missions News Summary," Press Release from SBC Foreign Mission Board, SBC, Richmond, Virginia, July 26-August 9, 1996.

[79] Jeff Giles, "Generalizations X," Newsweek, 6 June 1994, 61.

[80] Margot Hornblower, "Great Xpectations ," Time, June 9, 1997. Reactions to this article reinforces the diverse nature of these folks as well as their strong rejection of stereotyping are seen in the letters to the editor section of Time, June 30, 1997, 149:26.

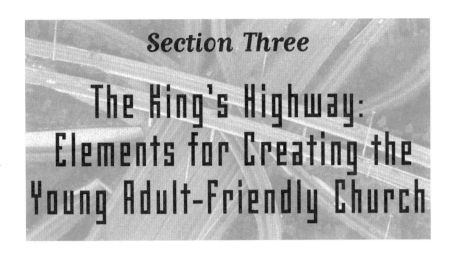

Section Three

The King's Highway: Elements for Creating the Young Adult-Friendly Church

1. The Issue at Hand

*"Therefore let us not judge one another anymore,
but rather determine this—not to put an obstacle or stumbling
block in a brother's way." Romans 14:13*

Purposefully or not, the church intersects young adults lives. That intersection happens as it annually celebrates the graduation of the latest group of 18-year-olds from high school and the youth group. It happens as worship attracts new visitors, or as church members witness to their friends and as normal outreach happens. The issue is not whether the church touches young adult lives, but what is it doing with those intersections it already has. That is the issue at hand.

The Great Commission

The church exists to make disciples of Jesus. Matthew 28:19-20 is its Great Commission to convert and disciple all nations. Acts 1:8 describes the progression of that effort. Witness is all inclusive. God expects the church to reach out to everyone everywhere. Just as the Gospel excludes no language or ethnic group, neither does it exclude any age group. Young adults fall well within the

range of both Matthew 28:19 and Acts 1:8. The church must focus some of its energy on this group, not because they are clam-
oring for attention, but because Jesus said for us to do it. It is a
factor of the church's obedience.

Obedience and Disobedience

Across the years the church has been obedient in this work. College-career or young single adults have always been included in
Sunday School and discipleship programs. Campus ministry efforts have flourished as local churches have supported denominational and para-church groups. As time passed, however, things
became unbalanced. Young adult ministry declined, while youth
ministry flourished. Today it is the rare church that lacks some
kind of junior high and high school youth ministry. Parents demand it, and provide the dollars to make it happen, including the
hiring of a salaried youth pastor. This is not so for the post-high
school graduate young adult.

High school graduation is a demarcation line. Seniors, once the
mainstay of the youth program, graduate to become people without a place. They might be tolerated for a couple of years as "at-
tachments" to the youth program, but then they must go away.
Somehow the parents of young teenage girls, for example, get
nervous when young adult males become too involved. The church
seems to expect their young adults to transition smoothly to adulthood, but forgets that life brings no smooth transitions. We have
already established that young adults have no experience with
the transitions going on within and about them. Like it or not,
the wise church will accommodate its expectations and ministry
to meet the needs of transitional young adults.

From Apathy to Attention

Christ expects it and young adults need it. So the local church must move from apathy to attention, from status quo to intentional, creative approaches to keep and reach young adults. The local church must seek to make itself "young adult user friendly." To do that might will take some adjustment of attitude, program and style. This can happen in any church, regardless of size, that has a will and a desire to do it.

2. *Their Dream Church*

Certain elements make up the "young adult user-friendly church." We discovered these elements by going directly to the source. We did the dangerous thing and asked some young adults what they wanted and needed from their church. We asked them several questions about the elements, tangible and intangible, that would make up their dream church, the church that would be most attractive to them as believers and young adults. With great unanimity they reflected the crying needs of their generation, and plainly stated what they needed from their church.

Their dream church is like the church they now attend, with some important adjustments. It is a church body of people of all ages, and backgrounds. Large size, however, is not important. Young adults prefer to worship with about 300 other folks. Any larger group becomes too impersonal. [2]

They recognize that their church will have a specific heritage, and doctrinal stance but do not consider that of first importance. For our respondents those aspects were givens. These young adults were asking nothing more of the church than what Christ meant for it to be in the first place.

Acceptance

Intangibles were foremost in their minds. Architecture, style, upkeep recede to the background. They want the church to be a place of love for God, and for people, a place of acceptance and warmth. One said, "The greatest intangible element, I feel, is to feel comfortable when you walk into a church."[3] Another suggested, "I want to be welcomed and accepted and treated as a member of the Body, as a vital part of the church."[4] Young adults will come to a church that welcomes, loves, and includes them as partners in the family. They are quick to express this feeling.

This acceptance has an edge, however. Those surveyed desire a church that recognizes their own unique life situation. They want a church that respects their newly acquired adult status, and treats them as adults (even if they sometimes do not act like it). They need recognition because of their own self-doubt.

> Practically, for the church to welcome me it needs to honor the truth I bring with me, welcome my energy, and bless my inexperience. For me there is nothing more discouraging and soul-sucking than entering a church and leaving without anyone saying hello, showing interest in me, or inviting me to get involved.[5]

Separation Yet Inclusion

Young adults want ministry, classes, and activities specifically for them, and desire nurture, and inclusion in the broader church life. Their dream church would demand service and responsibility from them, while at the same time taking their life situations and transitions into consideration. It would offer them many different opportunities for involvement at times more attuned to their life schedules, and not just on Sunday morning. One suggested:

The church would recognize that we are the future of the church. We would be recognized as an integral part of the body and would be encouraged to participate in the church ministry activities. The favorite words of the 18-24-year-old Christians are not "Cool, dude!", but "God loves!"[6]

Relevance and Excellence

The dream church is forward looking. It brings biblical truth to bear on contemporary situations. In the midst of its traditions, and sometimes in spite of them, the church will speak the truth in love. It will have an attractive and vibrant delivery system for the gospel. Church activities and worship will be done with excellence.

Their dream church will act like it is moving toward the twenty-first-century, rather than trying to hold on to the relics of a dead, but recent past. It will show this movement by a creative use of the technology with which young adults are so familiar. This church will include those young adults in the use of that technology, whether it be for word processing, video displays, or sound equipment.

Young adults will not tolerate boring preaching. Neither will they tolerate ignorant sounding, sweat-dripping, guilt-inducing, arm-flailing yelling. They desire their pastors to preach warm, vibrant, interesting and personal Biblical messages that clearly describe how the Scriptures apply to the needs and hurts of their lives.

Vibrant Worship

The worship service will be relational in tone, focusing on pertinent needs and issues. Its message of hope and acceptance will be matched by acceptance being modeled by church members.

Relationship with people would be secondary to relationship to God. The experience must have a sense, a tinge of the transcendent and mystery of God.

Because young adults like options, the church will provide worship and study at a variety of times. Because their likes and dislikes are as varied as there are kinds of people, the worship format of the church need not be different from its regular or "traditional" style.[7] Churched young adults also like variety and options. They appreciate a blend of old and new Christian music, with hymns mixed with contemporary scripture songs. While they will tolerate plain pianos and organs, keyboards, drums and guitars played well and in contemporary style are their church instruments of choice. Whatever the style, the music must be upbeat and well done.

3. Specifics

The young adults of the survey listed some specific things they want from the church, a church that they know consists of their parents and elders and younger brothers and sisters.

· They desire a church where older people go out of their way to include them and "hang out" with them once in a while.

· They desire a church that respects, trains and loves them.

· They are looking for the church to involve and give them responsibility in every aspect of church life.

· Their dream church speaks the truth of the Gospel to them and the issues of their lives, starting from their point of view.

- They desire a church with flexibility of schedule, and a multiplicity of opportunities.

- They want their church to be "prophetic" by guiding them as they seek to lead their lives in society, first as human beings and secondly as Christians.

- Their dream church will actively intentionally seek them out and try to bring them in. It will pay attention to them. Most importantly, it will have a pastor who is their friend, and advocate; who leads the church to seek, win and involve them.

4. Starting Points for the Church

The dream church survey, and others like it, help us discover the starting points of a young adult-friendly church. Any church can become young adult-friendly. It does not have to betray its own history or traditions. In reality, it just has to be in the process of becoming the church Jesus intended in the first place. This kind of church will almost instinctively, but surely intentionally do and be some of the following things:

- It will recognize that young adults are truly adults and need to be treated as such.

- It will understand that young adults need connection and "family" desperately, and will work very hard at providing the family and acceptance they need.

- It will recognize that as true adults young adults need to "own" the ministry and organization. It will insist that young adults take responsibility for the work and success of any church ministry to young adults. It will be willing to allow success or failure, calling the young adults to responsible accountability for both.

· It will recognize that they need a non-parental authority figure, and are willing to allow such a one into their lives. The young adult-friendly church will actively seek such a person or persons to work with and minister to young adults. It will put as much intentionality into young adult ministry as it puts into youth ministry.

· It will recognize that for young adults, while it is not a sin to be traditional, it is a sin to be boring.

· It will boldly tell the unvarnished, biblical truth about God, persons, and moral and cultural issues, but it will do so with the utmost Christian love.

· It will value persons and relationships above programs, and use programs as tools to reach persons for Christ and build relationships both inside and outside of the church.

· Its leaders will recognize that their own worship and even "cultural" bias does not automatically coincide with that of young adults. Its leaders will be willing to suspend their own bias to accommodate that of young adults. If they are working with churched young adults, they will, in turn, help them accommodate their own biases enough to become part of a multigenerational church family. [9]

There are no guarantees. There are many variables. Young adults are free agents acting, or not acting, for reasons often beyond their own understanding. They will choose or react according to the choices they make and the attitudes they have.

Acting to reach this generation is not, however, their responsibility. It is the responsibility of the church as the body of Christ. It is the Great Commission mandate. It is right. The church is the evangelistic and disciple-making aggressor. To be anything less is to deny its birthright. Like the apostle Paul, the church and those individual believers who make it up must become all things to all men in order to win some. To do less is to deny its birthright. To do less is disobedience.

[1]Mark Wyatt, "Young adults describe 'dream church,'" *The California Southern Baptist*. November 4, 1993, p. 5. Based on research conducted in 1993 by the College and Singles Ministries Department, California Southern Baptist Convention, Fresno, California, Dr. Dale G. Robinson, director.
[2]George Barna, The Invisible Generation, p.165.
[3]Jenness Park Focus Group, July, 1995.
[4]Jenness Park Focus Group, July, 1995.
[5]Jarrett Kerbel, "Generation's Faith," Sojourners, November, 1994, 15.
[6]Jenness Park Focus Group, July, 1995.
[7]Craig Kennet Miller, Post Moderns (Nashville, TN.: Discipleship Resources, 1996), p. 176.
[8]See George Barna, The Invisible Generation.
[9]Marve Knox, "Generations' tug-of-war pulls on churches," *Baptist Standard,* vol. 108. no. 37. September 11, 1996, p. 2.

Section Four

The Leaders' Map Book

"Set up for yourself roadmarks, place for yourself guideposts; Direct your mind to the highway, the way by which you went."
Jeremiah 31:21

No weekend road warrior can adequately minister to young adults. Not just any conscript has what it takes. Not only must you teach them the Bible, you must invest yourself in them. Young adults need Ezekiel 22:30 people, individuals who will step into the gap to meet their needs, address their issues and "save their land." They need leaders of character who reflect the traits they desire for themselves; mentors with a compatibility of spirit who will nurture their own spirits into maturity.

As there are intersections where young adult reality meets the gospel, there are also specific routes for achieving ministry with young adults. Take these routes and you have a lively, effective ministry. Forget any one of them, and you deprive yourself of opportunities and blessing.

Route 1
Heart - A Divine Calling

A Heart for Ministry

Courage and fortitude are two qualities needed to minister to young adults. Courage, however, is not the first route to effective ministry. Having the "heart" for it is. If you have a heart for this, your deepest concern will be young adults. Your grandest passion, after that for God and your family, will be a passion for young adults. You will thirst to see them know Jesus as Savior and Lord. You will hunger for them to mature as believers. You will ache for them to find fulfillment in relationships with their parents and peers, and crave that they succeed in life. You will push, press and demand that they live to their potential, courageously holding them accountable in the face of anger, rejection and apathy.

If you have no heart, no passion for young adults, no love for what they are and can become, then do not even try. They will see you for the sham you are. If you do have "heart," however, who knows? God may let you join him in his grand work with young adults. He may call you to ministry with them.

How does this passion begin? What are the motivating forces that cause an older believer to want to love and teach young adults? We can list a few, realizing that those same forces are at work in calling anyone to ministry, yet are especially needful for young adults.

The Heart of God

Passion for young adults began in God's own heart in the time before time. It began as He saw humanity fall into rebellion. It began as He sent His Son to die for the sins of the world. Young adults are part of God's heart because they are part of his beloved human creation, made in His image, for the express purpose of fellowship with him. Young adults are part of the world God loved so much that he sent his only begotten son. To exclude them from our seeking, witnessing and evangelism, either by intent or default, is to shame the heart of God.

Obedience to the Call of God

Passion begins with obedience. It may be a basic obedience to the command in James 4:17 *(KJV)*: "To him that knows to do good, and does it not, it is sin." It may be obedience to an Isaiah-like call with a response of "here I am, send me." Perhaps obedience comes as you open your spiritual eyes, see God at work in young adults around you and join Him in that vital work. Somehow God calls and you answer Him in the only correct way for a believer, in obedience and faith.

Make no mistake, you must have a sense of call in your passion. Without it, you are nothing more than a do-gooder. You may be successful for a while, but you will not have a true ministry. Heart and call are inseparable. Both provide the stamina and consistency the ministry demands. God must give you the heart as he calls you to service and you obey.

The Need is Lifted

A church leader may catch the vision that young adults ought to be one of the church's priorities. They would "lift up" the need for someone to lead out in the ministry. Someone could announce this at a prayer meeting or some strategy planning time. God may speak through the lifting of the need directly to you and call you into this kind of service.

You are Recruited

A church leader may enlist you to fill an empty spot in the Sunday School roster. They need a young adult teacher, and you are it. This may start out as a routine, but temporary assignment. If that is all it remains, you should quit at the end of the first lesson. If it is merely a job you will be ineffective. You had better quit, or the class will quit you. If, on the other hand, you catch a vision for who those young adults are and can become, you just might find real fulfillment and ministry.

Personal Experience As a Young Adult Yourself

Many respond to God's call because some older adult invested in them when they were young adults. College students in strong campus ministry programs often feel called to work with their peers. This can reassert itself later on as young adults marry and seek a spot in church life that fits them. Folks who had a good campus ministry experience or strong mentoring themselves see the value of young adult ministry because their own lives were changed.

A Vested Interest

Some will take on young adult work because all of a sudden they have a vested interest in it. Their own children and others in the youth group are graduating, and face a Sunday School situation that will not meet their needs. These folks have likely been working with the youth group. They already know the "kids" and have an established rapport. They understand the issues and the unique needs of that particular group. Having a vested interested is a strong motivator for older adults working with young adults. It can also be the starting place in a response to God's call. Whatever the reason, persons accepting leadership in a church ministry to young adults take on a divine task.

Combination of Gift and Interest

You may not be aware that you have the ability or personality type to work with young adults until you start to study the appropriate scriptures. You do that, and discover that you indeed have the gifts of teaching, hospitality, service. Then you discover that young adults are the perfect people to serve with your specific combination of spiritual gifts, talents, personality and love. You respond in obedience, and a fruitful ministry is born.

Route 2
Character-A Dedicated Personal Life

Nothing attracts young adults like consistency of character. You will succeed as you develop and strengthen the character traits listed below. If you do not, you will be wasting your time working with young adults.

Commitment

Commitment implies a pledge to stick with what you have determined to do or be. It is the living out of that pledge on a daily basis. Commitment is inner character and outward action. One follows the other. Good intention without commensurate action is lip service, which God hates. In Isaiah 29:13 he condemns Israel because "they honor me with their lip service, but they remove their hearts far from me." He led the apostle James to proclaim, "faith without works is dead" *(2:26)*.

There are four primary objects of commitment. First, <u>God</u> demands first place in your life. You must experience salvation and desire to serve Him. Then, you must desire to share His love with others. Without this prime commitment, nothing else is possible.

Second, you must be committed to your <u>family</u>, to spending time with them, to loving your spouse and children, to discipline and guidance for your children. Young adults need the quality role model of good family life.

Third, you must be committed to the <u>church</u>. This involves a commitment to the church's goals and purposes, to regular attendance, to financial support, and to an attitude of respect and support of the pastor. It does not mean an abdication of your own integrity, however, in various church matters.

Fourth, you must be committed to young adults, to their well being and growth. You must love them and demand the best from them. Your entire demeanor should say you want to spend time with them beyond Sunday morning Bible study, or worship attendance. You must accept them, warts and all.

Vision

Vision has to do with purpose and direction. Young adult leaders need to know what they want to see God accomplish in the lives of their young adults, and begin working and planning to those ends. Having sensed God's direction, they then need to share it with the group clearly, regularly and often. Vision must be articulated again and again. Then they must implement it and measure the value of each activity or project or work by that vision.

The reason that leaders must have, articulate, and repeat the vision for the group is very simple: a visionary leader generates confidence in others. If there is any one major thing young adults need it is confidence in leaders. They lack this quality in many areas of their lives, and to have it will strengthen them. A defined and repeated vision gives young adults the security from which to launch their own vision, and the training they need to pull it off.

The vision must fit within certain parameters.
1. It must be biblical. No vision of ministry ought to exist without squaring with the guidelines of the Bible.

2. It must also match that of the church as a whole. Young adult ministry is a function and ministry of the church and must be

compatible with it. When the vision of the young adult matches that of the church, both the church and the ministry are strengthened. Remember it is the church to whom God gave the keys to the Kingdom, not one age group or section of the church.

Experience

Experience implies a certain skill level. This does not necessarily mean that a leader should have previous young adult experience before he starts to work with young adults. That might be too much of a catch-22 situation. It does mean that leaders need to have a successful track record in people and leadership skills. It means that leaders know about life, and have developed coping skills. It means that leaders have developed patience and openness. It means that they are not rank amateurs. Young adult leaders need at least to be able to share from personal experience rather than often untried head knowledge.

Teachability

When something stops growing, it is dead. When a thing is dead, it decays, and stinks. The same is true of you as leaders. Growth, expressed in the continuing ability to be taught something new is a prime characteristic. People who are unteachable, who are not open to considering new ideas, will never be successful leaders, especially of young adults.

Teachability means that you can gain from your students. Young adults have much to teach older people. If you are open to humble learning you will reap great harvests of love and relationships. Being teachable adds value to the young adults, and strengthens their own sense of self worth.

Second, it means you can learn from your mistakes, and avoid the various pitfalls experienced by others. Thirdly it means that you can benefit from the successes of others, and by learning of those successes, can in turn benefit your own group.

Genuineness and Authenticity

Several words describe this most valued character trait: honesty, truthfulness, transparency, authenticity, genuineness. You, as leaders, must be people of truth and integrity. You must "walk the talk," accurately reflecting the truths you teach. Honesty is not perfection. Young adults understand that no one is really perfect. They would rather their leaders admit their limitations than try to act like they have none. Hypocrisy is out. Truthfulness is in.

Authenticity involves transparency. It is admitting failure, and asking for forgiveness when necessary. It means actually being and doing what you teach. This brutal self honesty is not without "danger" for you, the leader. Being transparent involves the risk of exposing everything you are to examination by others. It involves treating people young enough to be your own children as equals and getting off any self-established -ivory towers. You must respect young adults, but in respecting them you will win them.

Persistent Aggressiveness

A key trait for any leader is persistence. With young adults it also involves aggressiveness. By virtue of their on-going transitions young adults are preoccupied and self-centered. They are easily distracted, pulled away from the best by the good. Their life stages makes them short-sighted, susceptible to spur-of-the-moment decisions. They forget long-scheduled responsibilities. Because of that, you must work hard to be included in your young adults' life-styles. It means you must insert yourself aggressively and persistently into their frame of reference. You are to be aggressive because other forces are vying for their attention, and persistent because the only way to etch yourself on a busy mind is by continuous and repetitious action.

Person-Centeredness

Persons must be your central concern. Your beliefs, thoughts
and actions must all be geared to influencing persons; teaching
persons; winning persons to Christ. You will act on your belief in
the value of those with whom you minister by spending time
with them, and paying attention to them. You will demonstrate
their worth by learning from them. Most importantly, you will
willingly and often put aside schedule, calendar and even well-
made plans because the needs of your young adults come first!

Personal Security

Scripture describes the Christian as possessing an armor of light,
a breastplate of righteousness, a helmet of salvation, a girdle of
truth. This armor serves to deflect the "fiery darts of the wicked"
and protects the believer from the attacks of Satan. For you this
armor means having a strong sense of self-worth, and personal
security, coupled with a high threshold for rejection and pain.
(Romans 13:12, Ephesians 6:10-18)

More than any group, young adults have a way of hurting those
who love them. As often as not, this hurt does not come because
of intentional meanness, but from their immaturity. You need to
have spirits large enough to overwhelm pettiness, ego-centrism
and arrogance. People who work with this group need to have the
patience of Job in the face of young adult turmoil.

There are many sources of distress for a leader. A young person
with great potential who squanders it, can hurt. Someone who
knows to live a moral life and does not can hurt. Your young
friend suddenly curses you out because you called him or her to
be accountable for the very thing they agreed to earlier. People
you gave responsibility did not follow through, and you have no
refreshments, or must do someone else's cleanup job.

If you do not have strong personal self-esteem, you will too soon burn out. If your sense of self worth is not founded on a true understanding that God is your only means of support, you will be "eaten alive" by the work.

Flexibility

A rubber band has two endearing qualities. One, it works best and most efficiently when it is stretched. Two, it is remarkably flexible. The rubber band is the symbol of young adult ministry because that work stretches those who do it, and demands they maintain an unusual amount of flexibility. The rubber band can continue to be stretched only as long as it is flexible. When it ceases to be flexible, it will crack, and ultimately break. While the rubber band's value is in its stretchability, the secret of its success is its flexibility.

Young adult habits, lifestyles, attitudes all demand flexibility in those who work with them. While "flakiness" is not next to Godliness, the smart leader will always realize its existence. Leaders who understand this will take have Plans B, C, and even D on the "back burner" and ready to go. Leaders who understand this will reap great rewards of relationship. They will be the recipients of the great love, trust and care that young adults are capable of sharing.

Those who do not understand the need for flexibility will find themselves ministering all alone, with no one in sight. I saw this happen one time. It had to do with a discussion about dancing. The issue then was not the rightness or wrongness of this now universally-practiced activity. The issue was getting the group to discuss the reasons for and against it in ways that would help them understand the problems and come to adult decisions. The discussion was not to be, however, because of the inflexibility of one of the older adult leaders. He was clearly against dancing, and stated so in no uncertain terms. Then he went on a verbal tirade against it in front of the group. Of course, that was the end of that chance for growth. In his inflexibility, he effectively poured ice cold water on the discussion, and erected barriers with his own young adults that most likely ruined his relationships with them.

This sad incident brings up an important issue for leaders. To reach young adults we must be willing submerge our own cultural and generational prejudices. We must be willing to stand apart from our almost "instinctual" values and lift up those things important to young adults. This means that we develop an insight into what is biblical, what is cultural and the ability to tell the difference.

Creativity

In young adult eyes it is a mortal sin to be boring. When anything or anyone has a reputation of being boring, that anything or anyone may as well give it up. If you are boring, young adults disappear. To combat that, young adult leaders need constantly to be seeking new and creative ways of relating to them. This is not novelty for novelty's sake, but rather an on-going search for ways and means of catching and holding their interest.

Creativity is a trait every leader must work hard to develop. Yes, creativity is an innate quality for some folks. But like any worthwhile goal, it is 10 percent inspiration and 90 percent perspiration. Leaders learn creativity by reading, studying and going to conferences. They catch it by seeking out and relating to other creative people. Creativity is the holy grail of quality leadership. Anyone who has and exercises it will draw others like a light draws moths.

Balance

Leaders with balance keep everything in perspective. You have a sense of rightness and propriety. You seldom go to extremes. You keep an equilibrium in your own life, and in the way you work with young adults. Having balance gives a leader the aura of maturity and wisdom. This is not a passive, "other worldly" attitude, but rather an intentional decision to avoid emotional, intellectual and spiritual extremes, while consistently ministering with your God-given passion.

Humor

If being boring is a mortal sin, being humorless will condemn you to some kind of young adult perdition. Humor is a major factor in winning friends, and influencing people. It is a key element is interesting presentations. Having a good sense of humor will earn any leader a great place in the hearts of young adults.

Humor should be gentle, and not biting. Wisely used, it will destroy barriers and win an audience and friends. Unwisely used, it can destroy people, and lose credibility. You must have a sense of humor. How else can you respond when your young friends super glue your favorite coffee cup to the wall, or when they string toilet paper all over the yard in the early morning hours? You must have a sense of humor, or you are dead in the eyes of young adults. You must even be glad of making yourself the object of some of that humor. After all, if you do you will never run out of material. Humor lets others know you are happy. What better way to demonstrate the love of Jesus, than to be happy and let others know it?

A Walk With God

The most important character trait for leaders to develop is really a habit. This is the habit, the discipline of maintaining a consistent, regular "walk with God." What this means is that leaders read and meditate on the Word of God. It means they seek God's guidance in the Scripture, and in prayer. It means they pray for themselves, their families, their church, and their young adults on a regular basis. It means putting into daily practice the ethical and moral instructions. Most of all, it means letting the Holy Spirit shine through their lives so that only Jesus is seen in the reflection.

Route 3
Discernment—An Informed Understanding of Young Adults

Effective ministry emerges from what you know and understand about young adults. The ministry is shaped by what they need and value. Their needs are discovered by knowledge of the demands of a sovereign God, as well as an understanding of human nature. Their values are discovered by observation and conversation with them.

Ministry informed by knowledge will have a specific shape. That shape will influence the approach you take and the elements you include. Knowledge-based ministry will be built on the foundation of evangelism. It will be supported by the pillars of biblical answers to life's issues and responsibility. It focuses specific desired outcomes for and with young adults as persons and in the group.

Evangelism
The primary need of any young adult is a personal relationship with Jesus Christ. That every member of the class or group come

to salvation is the highest need, and requires your highest priority. You as a leader need to have this as a passion of ministry. It must permeate everything you plan and do. The salvation of young adults must inform and shape your teaching, counseling and actions. This means you must know each member's spiritual condition, and pray consistently for the salvation of those who are lost. It means that you can and must be blatant in your sharing of the gospel in a kind, considerate and sensitive way. The old adage, "If at first you don't succeed, try, try again," applies here. Then as you love and witness, the group will catch that zeal and desire. In this, as in all things, the leader must lead and be the model for loving and action.

Biblical Answers

Young adults ask the hard questions. They also respect the strong answer. That answer must, however, be based first on your relationship with them, and a tenth of a point below that, on the truth of Scripture. In matters of ethics, especially, you must be ready with truthful, biblical answers, answers that speak directly to their need and with gospel authority.

But, just what constitutes a "biblical" answer? A biblical answer is what the Bible actually says. Sometimes the instruction is so clear that you cannot miss it. "Thou shalt not kill" is pretty obvious. A biblical answer also takes the complete teaching of scripture into consideration. Sometimes, there is no simple biblical answer. You must just refer to pertinent passages, and give your best interpretation.

It is appropriate to give answers supported by scripture, but be sure that you are not taking those passages out of context. Prooftexting does violence to the truth of scripture because in one sense it makes you ruler over scripture, rather than letting scripture rule you.

My favorite bad example of proof-texting is the suggestion that the scripture encourages suicide (which it most certainly does not). This line of thinking goes like this: "Judas went away and hanged himself," *(Matt. 27:5)*; "Go, and do the same," *(Luke 10:37)*; "What you do, do quickly," *(John 13:27)*. Following these truthful scriptures, as outlined, you might be persuaded that Christ commands you to follow Judas' example. When, however, you read these verses in context you discover no such command. You find that while the John and Matthew verses do relate to Judas, they refer to different situations. The verse from Luke is not even connected.

Give biblical, truthful answers to any questions or issues. Be sure your answers reflect timeless and eternal truths, not pet interpretations or personal reactions, for or against, current styles or clothing fads. For example, it is a very '90s "thing" for young adult males to wear one or more earrings, mostly in their left earlobe, but often in both ears. This fad, repelling to many older adults, seems at the very least rebellious, and at the worst totally immoral. It is one of the fads that pass through the population, like cutting the belt loops off my jeans, when I was in high school. Earrings for men may or may not be a long-term item in American culture.

Freedom and Responsibility

As young adults do the ministry, and as they experience mentoring, they will need a clear field in which to do their work and live their lives. Older leaders must not monopolize the action or seek to control it. Since young adults often grew up with a great deal of self-dependence, they value it. There will be a positive response whenever they receive the freedom to succeed or fail on their own.

Route 4
Wisdom - A Strategic Plan

A strategy is a game plan. It is the chosen path leaders take to accomplish their objectives. In relation to young adults, a strategy is the plan you will follow to accomplish your goal of winning, nurturing and sending them in Jesus' name. A well-defined strategy is appealing to them. It can catch their imagination, and draw great levels of commitment from them. It gives them something solid to grasp, when everything else around them seems so fluid. You cannot work with young adults haphazardly. While they may not hold themselves to any kind of consistent structure, they demand it in older leaders.

The Value of Strategy
A defined strategy is the answer to a mind-and-body-numbing "seat of the pants" approach. It allows leaders to focus on ministry rather than mechanics. It "frees up" leaders to focus both on persons and the broad direction of their work without being drowned in last minute details. A strategy defines the kind of events and projects a ministry will have. The strategy employed must fit the personalities of both leaders and group members and must synchronize with the goals and objectives of the church.

Twelve Elements of a Strategic Plan
However a strategy looks at the end, I believe it should include some specific elements. Leaders will develop strategies in each of the following areas to have a balanced and potentially successful ministry. These areas relate to both the leader's personal life, and the actual "doing" of the work with young adults.

1. Churchmanship

Any strategy to reach young adults must be grounded in churchmanship, that love, loyalty and connection to the church. The goal is to establish, define, and continue the ministry's inseparable and organic connection with the local church that actually does the work of the kingdom.

Young adult ministry exists to achieve the ends, goals and purposes of the church of which it is a part. From the church's perspective, the young adult ministry is its method of reaching persons for Christ in that age group. Without that connection, guidance and direction, any ministry will be reduced to the level of a social organization that happens to do religious things. The strategy of the young adult leader must include ways to help the young adults love and support the church. It must involve honoring the church and pastor, and promoting loyalty to the church, not as an institution, but as the Bride of Christ.

2. Investment in Lives

Conversely, leaders need constantly to remind the church that its long term investment in young adults will pay off in the future. Leaders will be the advocates and catalysts for young adult involvement in the church, helping them obtain and carry out church responsibilities. Leaders will include young adults as full members of the church family. They will also make sure that young adults pull their fair share of the church's ministry and work.

3. Intentionality

There are at least two sure-fire ways to guarantee an organic connection between the young adult ministry and the church. The first is that this ministry is an *intentional, natural part* of the church's world evangelism strategy. The traditional Sunday

School approach, for example, is to be age-graded. College-Career/Young Adult Sunday School classes speak to the built-in organization of Sunday School. Such classes or groups also speak to the need to be relevant, and to build around "affinity groupings," that is, to build groups of persons with like needs, concerns and issues.

4. Budget Money

The second sure-fire way to guarantee organic connection is inclusion in *the budget* of the church. This means that young adult leaders are always aggressive in asking for dollars to do the work, and are effective in spending the dollars they do have. A church that budgets for young adults is investing in the lives of persons at a time when their energies are most open to direction and guidance. A church that invests in young adult ministry is assuring its own future, and protecting the investments it has made in the children and youth who are quickly becoming young adults.

5. Continuous Communication

Continuous communication is the grafting material that makes the ministry integral to the church. Leaders need to be constantly aware of telling their story to the church family whenever and wherever possible. Communication takes place simply, by the sharing of a prayer request to the support team or the pastor or to the prayer meeting group on Wednesday night. It takes place when young adults share testimonies of God's grace in their lives, and when they share needs or opportunities with the whole church. Communication occurs when articles and announcements appear in the church newsletter and in the Sunday bulletin. People catch a feel for the work's importance as young adults exert real church leadership, and gently remind the church of who and what they are.

Educating the church about young adults is a constant task. It demands finesse, skill, thoroughness and great humility. Successful communication, however, requires a dogged determination and conviction that only by communication can a connection be kept strong and vibrant.

6. A System of Personal Support for the Leaders

A valuable strategy for leaders is to set up a personal support system separate from the ministry itself. Face it. Young adults are high maintenance individuals. They need, want and demand high touch, close personal interaction and personal attention. Leaders only have so much of themselves to give. An on-going process of giving and interacting is exhausting. Leaders need a support system to fall back upon when energy is exhausted, and time has run out.

A support system should be many-faceted, filled with alternatives, and fail-safes. It should be varied. Like Brer' Rabbit's briar patch, it needs to be a jumble of protected pathways to which the leader can retreat for safety and renewal. It may have some or all of the following elements.

Someone To Turn To

Everyone needs the clarity of insight gained from a friend's listening ear and new perspective. As leaders, you need the benefit of someone else's support, insight and guidance. This someone would have your trust and the freedom to be brutally honest. That individual should know how to ask you the right questions. He or she should have the freedom to call your favorite presuppositions into question.

Having such a person available is vital to a leader's mental health. You could call this person (or couple if you and your spouse are ministering to young adults together) your "buddy," "spiritual advisor," "mentor," "partner," "accountability partner" or "pastor." The name is less important than the function. When you need a prayer partner, a shoulder to cry on, that "someone" is there. When you need to vent frustrations about the work or specific young adults, that someone will be there. Perhaps you will visit that person face to face, perhaps it will be by phone or e-mail. In turn you will listen without defensiveness, but with openness and a willingness to learn. You will reap the insight gained by someone distanced from your situation, someone with different experience.

This someone might be a friend, or a pastor, or another staff member of your church. It might be a local campus minister, or one of the state denominational staff. Regardless of who it is, the first strategic decision you make in building support for your ministry is to find "someone to turn to."

A Ministry Support Team

The next strategy is to amplify the "someone to turn to" idea in the form of a "ministry support team." Enlist a group of persons from the church to support you and your ministry. They will not need much organization. The more informally you do this, the better. You may never gather them all together at one time. You will need to share your prayer concerns, and needs and issues with each one. These people will be your friends and even the focus of your accountability.

a. What It Does

Corporately and individually, members of your support team will be your prayer partners, advocates and helpers. They will pray regularly for you, speak out for your ministry in the many forums of church life and provide you with the mentoring you need to grow. Your support group will be the listening ear and the solid shoulder you lean on in times of frustration, joy or sorrow. It can be your prayer strength.

b. Who should be on it?
This team can also be your leadership seed bed. It is that place where you first plant those you are nurturing to become young adult leaders on their own. In this aspect you would find others in the church who just might be candidates for your ministry job sometime in the future. These might be recent graduates from the young adult ministry, or "fresh from college" young married adults. Parents of high school juniors and seniors soon to enter the adult world are prime candidates, as are long-time youth leaders who are ready for a change, but not ready to give up ministry.

Your team members should be persons of respect and influence in your congregation. They may or may not be elected church leaders. In reality you should enlist anyone who wants to help you. There are, however, those individuals who want to help you. Senior adult prayer warriors are likely candidates. They have the heart to pray and love you. If you ask them to pray regularly for you, you are giving them a great gift. They can be the listening ear and the solid shoulder you need.

People with ministry experience are potential team members. These are folks who themselves experienced campus ministry or a good young adult or single adult group. They already have good feelings about your ministry, and often really would like to help. Because of their experience they have some idea of your problems and issues. They understand the complexities of working with young adults, and will remember the life they led as young adults, not so long ago.

Elected church leaders should also be on your team. This may be a deacon, or elder, or Sunday School Director, or other recognized church leader. These folks are already in position to render needed aid and support. They can give public, verbal credence to the idea of your work, as well as to the activities you do.

7. Appropriate Leadership

Persons called on to work with young adults have a responsibility to add value to them. This can be done by exerting their leadership in attractive and positive ways, by leading in ways that releases them to be creative. Any leadership style that adds value to young adults and helps them lead is appropriate for this ministry.

Remember the basic principle. While you may be a teacher or program planner in your church, you may or may not be a real leader. Leadership is mainly influence, not position. It must involve others in the training, the planning and the doing.

8. A Vision for Ministry

Wisdom is best expressed in the belief that God can accomplish mighty things with young adults. Leaders who catch that vision for ministry will have motivation and power as they do it. Those leaders must articulate that vision, that dream. They must think through what they will want to help God accomplish, and will spell it out in writing for themselves, for the church, and for young adults. This way they will become loud sounding trumpets of God's direction and care.

9. Spiritual Growth

Leading is like driving a car that runs great with a full tank and enough octane. If the tank runs dry, the car stops dead. It is important for leaders constantly to fuel themselves spiritually for their work. Running out of energy in this work is akin to running out of gas going up a hill. All you can do is roll backwards.

God is always willing to fill us up with spiritual energy, but it is our task to provide the opportunities for that to happen. We have to slow down long enough to pull over close to the fueling point, so He can renew our strength.

10. Personal Bible Study

At the heart of letting God empower us is the discipline of personal Bible study and scripture memorization. This is not the regular preparation you do to teach Sunday School, or a weekday Bible study. This is personal, private scripture reading and prayer. It is a process in which you allow God to speak through the written Word to the situations and problems of your personal life and ministry.

There is no one "right" way to do personal Bible study. There are many options or methods from which to choose. The most important factor, however, is the intentionality and consistency of your devotion time.

A second factor is that you then meditate on what you read, and make mental application of those verses in your own circumstances. At your request, the Lord will open your memory and understanding. He will help you apply those words to your situation, and strengthen you in life and ministry. This kind of directed thinking will give you a spiritual foundation from which to minister.

You will develop resources that will spring to mind when you are teaching or leading or dealing with difficult questions. If you work with computers, you know the truth of the axiom, "GIGO," "garbage in, garbage out." The reverse is also true: "GSIGSO," "good stuff in, good stuff out." When you fill your mind with the "good stuff" of God's word, then it will come back to you at appropriate times and in powerful ways. Remember God's promise that His word "shall not return to me empty." *(Isaiah 55:11)*

11. Intellectual Growth

You as a leader grow in effectiveness when spiritual preparation combines with mental preparation and skill development. You are being asked to have or gain skills as a personnel manager, teacher, leader, biblical scholar, counselor and mentor. Each can be a full-time career demanding higher education. You will need to exercise some of those skills as a lay person. God, the church and those with whom you minister call on you to function with expertise and knowledge. How are you to do that? Well, sometimes, it just involves your own common sense and personal experience. Other times common sense is not quite enough. You discover the need for further training, or a review of the basics. You discover that young adults are challenging you to learn more, and grow as a person and leader. So what do you do?

The answer is simple. You take advantage of opportunities for formal and informal education in planned, intentional ways. If you stagnate, you die. If you do not fill up your mental tank as well as your spiritual one, you will lose the "racer's edge" you need. So, whenever one of these avenues of learning comes along, take it and use it to your advantage.

The Avenue of Reading

The first avenue of learning is plain, simple reading. The wealth of printed material on subjects of importance to young adult leaders is untold. You can read material to any depth or detail. The bibliography at the end of this book (and often at the end of any good book) is a good place to start in a planned program of reading and study. Religious book store catalogues can show the latest books available.

Leaders of young adults need to read widely, not necessarily deeply. Deep, detailed reading comes later with the discovery of areas of interest and need. Bible knowledge, history and background are a good place to start, as is Christian doctrine. Studying these subjects will give you a foundation for teaching and provide a ready reservoir of responses to questions and situations. Christian ethics and history will also give a good foundation. Sunday School teachers need a constant update on teaching methods and skills, as well as the insight and perspective given by reading Christian history and biography. Some study in learning theories and style is very important.

There is a great deal being written, both secular and Christian, about the so-called Baby Buster generation. Titles of some of the most important books are found in the bibliography. These books as well as pertinent articles, can be of great help in figuring out what young adults are thinking and doing. They will also help you anticipate the issues your young adults will deal with, and what your response can be.

Do not neglect recreational reading either! This is where you take mental vacations from the difficulties of life. You can learn a great deal about people by reading a good spy novel, or adventure story, science fiction, or mystery. This kind of reading rests your mind and maybe even brings new insights. A great by-product of recreational reading is that you just might even come up with a few good illustrations to liven up your teaching.

Magazines are valuable too. You could go broke on subscriptions. Be selective in what you purchase. *Reader's Digest* is a good place to start. After all, preachers get most of their jokes from that magazine, why not you too!? General interest magazines like *Smithsonian, National Geographic, Popular Science, Popular*

Mechanics, are all fun to read or at least glance at the pictures. There are any number of religious magazines of value to young adult leaders.

A thoughtful trip to the public library and quality bookstore can help you discover available titles. Be warned, however, that much that is available, even in the Christian bookstores, is of passing value and short-term interest. Identify and search for favorite authors. As you browse, notice the footnotes and bibliographies to discover whom everyone else quotes. Then go buy that book. If you do, you will get right to the main expert in any area.

Reading is itself a discipline, like sports, or scripture memorization. It must be practiced. The good news about reading is that most of us already have some grasp of it. Like anything else, however, practice makes perfect. You read for the knowledge and understanding you gain, the enjoyment you receive, or the skill you develop.[1] Leaders who read will enhance their ministry skills. They will provide themselves with readily useable resources for speaking and counseling. Reading brings knowledge, and with it power.

The Avenue of Participation

The second avenue is to discover and attend training events geared to expand your knowledge and skill level. Many religious groups, Southern Baptists especially, provide general and age-group-specific training for Sunday School teachers and ministry leaders. These events happen at local, regional, statewide and national levels throughout the year and provide quality, inexpensive training. Attendance at these events exposes you to the expertise and experience of others, as well as the newest printed material in the area you are studying.

Knowing about conferences and workshops is a constant, but not impossible adventure. Be sure that your pastor and Sunday School leadership are aware that you want to know about them. Pay attention to your church bulletin. Get acquainted with a professional church staff member with responsibilities for young adults or single adults who can share information with you.

The local, or state administrative offices of your denomination or church can keep you informed about conferences they provide. Make sure you are on their mailing lists to receive that information. Subscribe to regional and state newsletters and newspapers. Religious publishing houses produce materials and provide training events to support that material, and are anxious for you to know about the events and to attend.

If you are one of the growing number of computer owners, you can go on-line on the Internet. A short search on your favorite navigator can uncover a host of religious websites ripe for investigation. For a quick start into ministry assistance, begin with http://sbc.com or http://csbc.com. See the appendices for a longer list of helpful web pages.

The Avenue of Hearing and Seeing

Modern technology enables us to learn while we listen. Audio tapes of lectures, sermons, discussions, or books being read are readily available. They bring information and inspiration to us at our convenience, and point of need. The same organizations who produce printed material often also produce audio tapes in support of their resources.

Seeing is also learning. This avenue of understanding young adults is extremely important because many of them learn this way first or best. First, see what they see. Be alert to the movies and television shows they watch, shows that describe the secular aspects of their generation. Watch MTV occasionally for a feel of what young adults are looking at, wearing or thinking. Your particular group of young adults may or may not reflect those values, but you can be sure they are being influenced.

Second, see what the experts are saying about them. Be alert to video teaching courses published by religious publishing houses. These tapes will either be recordings of entire presentations, or will be learning aids for courses available for use in the church or for personal study.

12. Leaders Not Lumps

It is possible to lead without developing leadership. It is possible to have a class or group of listeners and lumps, but listeners and lumps soon lose interest and move to richer pastures. Neglecting leadership development verges on the unbiblical. The command to make and teach disciples is clear. Making leaders is also a part of that. The truly successful ministry produces confident leaders. It draws from among its participants persons able to give leadership, to use their giftedness, and to lead out later in life.

Young adults need to be convinced of their value by being brought into leadership. Ministry happens best with the participants are givers as well as takers, when they really "own" the ministry. Leadership development needs to continue always, because people are transient in nature. It is a process of growth, without which the ministry weakens.

One benefit of working with young adults is that they are truly adults. They are mobile self-starters with their own resources. Since they have a strong desire for recognition and adult status, they can and must be recruited and trained for leadership. They can be given responsibility and held accountable. When older leaders give leadership away to young adults, the burden is lightened

and the work amplified. There is the risk that some will be irre-
sponsible, but that is the risk leaders always take, regardless of
the age of their group.

First, discover natural leaders. This happens through observation, acquaintance and the giving of responsibilities. Those who
follow through with their responsibilities consistently and with
quality are likely good leadership material. Sometimes you have
to apply some "sanctified coercion" to get things done, to encourage them to follow through on commitments and responsibilities. If this is done, however, the young adult is stretched, the
job is accomplished. Just fixing the coffee on Sunday mornings
on a consistent basis may reveal a potential leader.

Next, thrust on the leaders the freedom to succeed or fail on their
own. The planning process becomes their responsibility. You
encourage them and expect them to participate, share ideas and
help make and carry out the decisions of the group.

Finally, you work with each leader in personal ways, spending
regular time with them to give guidance and suggestions. A talk
over lunch would do, or a more formal private meeting. The content of these times should involve a personal discipling process
and ministry planning. The discipleship time can include Bible
study or checking each other's scripture memorization. The ministry planning time includes discussion about work or projects
going on in the ministry for which that leader is responsible. Such
meetings give occasion for a better personal acquaintance and
friendship, as well as the chance to teach, train and reflect.

Route 5
Conduct - A Relational Style

If you want to reach young adults, you must act like it. Every behavior will be geared to that end. Your "style" of ministry will communicate to young adults that you love them and want to know them personally. What constitutes a relational style? The following statements try to define that.

Relational leaders are sensitive to young adult culture.

You will seek to discover and understand the unique features of young adult culture and try to accommodate to it. You will also have a clear understanding of your own cultural biases and will not try to impose the values and ideas of your generation on this one. You will, however, help young adults clarify the difference between changing trends and eternal biblical realities.

Relational leaders take initiative in building relationships.

Personal relationships begin in your heart. They flow from your passion to share Jesus with young adults. You initiate each action. You intentionally seek to become friends with your young adults. It may mean going out of your way to visit with them on their "turf", or subjecting yourself to uncomfortable noise levels. It may mean suspending your prejudices long enough to hear what they are really saying. You will be willing to share genuinely of yourself to earn the privilege of them sharing themselves with you. Relational leaders listen with an intensity, and give advice only after deep listening. Most of all, you "exude" the desire for relationship. You understand the homespun philosophy, "To have friends, you have to be one first."

Relational leaders practice lifestyle evangelism.

Lifestyle evangelism is at the heart of relationship building. This means that you bear witness to Christ with your entire life. It is "living for Jesus a life that is true." Everything you do in work or play or family life witnesses to Jesus' love. This kind of evangelism, however, is more than living a godly life. It is taking advantage of your opportunities for verbal witness and praying for boldness to ask the strong commitment questions.

Relational leaders spend personal time mentoring and discipling young adults.

We understand that young adults want independence. We also understand that they are smart enough to realize that they could use the knowledge and wisdom other adults have. They will respond to personal one-on-one relationships with older adults, relationships that take place regularly and formally, or sporadically and informally. Wise leaders actively look for those times to meet with young adults individually for personal or spiritual growth. This may be a regular personal meeting with organizational officers or leaders. It may be a seeking out of persons with untapped potential. Leaders become "brokers" in relationships by intentionally connecting older adults who have skills, with the younger adults who want those particular skills. We can draw persons closer to Jesus Christ as we meet with them for personal prayer and Bible study.

There is an interesting side effect of the mentoring opportunities for the older adult leaders. They will able to exert positive parenting influence at a time when relationships with real parents are at risk. It has to do with where the young adults "are" in relation to their own parents. Often, they cannot for some reason adequately communicate with their parents, or there is conflict as one wants independence and the other just will not let go.

You can become for young adults' "non-threatening authority figures," persons who know what parents know, but who do not represent constricting parental authority. This is a great service you can perform. You become a bridge person between the time young adults rebel against parental authority and "ignorance," and the time they realize that their parents really do have some sense after all.

We have said this ministry is intensive. It is intensive because to be successful older leaders must go one-on-one with younger ones, so that the younger ones can grow and mature. Hmmm! Isn't that what Jesus did with the Twelve, and Barnabas did with Saul, and Lois and Eunice and Paul did with Timothy?

Relational leaders make group interaction happen.

Part of the relational leaders' strategy is to provide multiple opportunities for young adults to interact with their friends. This may be informal, through some spontaneous after church or week night activities generated by word of mouth. It may be through creative Bible teaching techniques, such as asking interactive questions, or using small task or brainstorming groups. Group interaction occurs as they are "held captive" in a van or bus on a trip to the mountains or the beach for a retreat, or to some conference or training event. The goal of the relational leader is to provide as many group opportunities for young adults to meet and connect. Do not worry about playing matchmaker. Young adults are quite capable of doing that on their own.

Relational leaders facilitate gender-specific activities.

This is an era when the differences between the genders are blurred, and when gender-appropriate behavior is questioned. It is important for the church and its young adult leaders to provide good models for biblically-based manhood and womanhood. Occasional gender-specific outings, Bible studies, fellowships, and even on-going Sunday School classes will help young adults as they struggle with appropriate gender behaviors. There is a freedom of discussion in gender-specific situations not possible in a co-ed environment. Friendships develop that will last a life time, and support other relationships from a gender-specific context. It is the nature of young adults, especially younger ones, to need a group of "buddies" and same-gender friends as support for moving into the mysteries of relationships with the other sex.

Relational leaders create a climate for spiritual growth.

A "climate for spiritual growth" occurs when you intentionally and verbally make it happen. When your speech promotes and calls for growth, it is more likely to happen. When you set the tone by your comments, people are given permission to grow. They come to expect growth as a natural expected outcome of participation in the ministry. You must confirm your words by action, by your own spiritual growth. This will prove your genuineness and trustworthiness. Creating a climate where spiritual growth happens requires skill and the use of some basic tools.

Bible Study

The first tool is to seek the whole counsel of God through serious Bible study.   Young adults need to know the facts of and about the Scripture. They need to understand how God acted throughout history to insure their salvation and the meeting of their deepest heartfelt needs. Biblical details will be relevant for young adults only as leaders show Scripture's relevance for life.

Since there seems to be a lack of general factual knowledge about the Bible, it is appropriate to teach some of the Bible facts along with the pertinent application. Teachers may need to help them learn the preliminary basics for Bible study. Such basics might include the number of books in the Bible, the names of all the books, learned by memory and in order. Introductory instruction in pronunciation of Bible names and places is appropriate as is helping them understand the geography and historical background of the Bible lands.

The rationale of learning these basics is simple. These basic truths are the foundation for all other knowledge. Without it there is a danger of incomplete understanding or misinterpretation. Persons not knowing the basics open themselves to the lies of false teachers teaching improper doctrine.

Spiritual Accountability

Leaders who create a climate for spiritual growth build in opportunities to implement spiritual accountability. You win for yourselves the right to hold others accountable for mutually-agreed spiritual goals and actions. You must wield such a privilege gently and cautiously. It is to be used infrequently and appropriately. Being a "non-threatening spiritual authority figure" means walking a tight rope of relationship, for the leader wants to influence, but does not want to be the subject of any negative anti-parent reaction.

Retreats and Trips

Retreats and trips provide the excuse and occasion for God to speak so young adults will hear. When young adults withdraw from the busyness of daily life into the isolation of a retreat, they find the occasion for spiritual growth. Retreats and trips provide extraordinary, quality opportunities for other good things to happen as well. Groups cement relationships through common experience. Personal relationships strengthen. Retreats allow each person time for quiet personal reflection, as well as the chance for group worship, play and fellowship, not to mention plain fun. And, the good thing about young adult retreats is that they need no chaperones. Because they are "of age" they act in reasonably adult ways, and they can provide their own transportation.

Using retreats and trips as a part of a ministry strategy will allow you the extra, concentrated time you need to become better acquainted with your young adults. It will give a unity to the group, and help it jell. Newcomers and incoming high school seniors can be invited along as a way of getting acquainted more quickly.

Missions/Ministry Trips and Projects

Mission trips and projects are a great way of moving the group's focus from themselves to others. They are the means of helping each young adult move from the theory of the Great Commission to its practice. The spirit of altruism can take on present, practical meaning as young adults engage in ministry to share the gospel. They will enhance their own self esteem as they help build a house, or church. At the same time, they have the opportunity to learn from each other and from older adults. They can be exposed to the needs of other people, and be pushed from their own selfishness to an understanding of what they really have. Mission or ministry experiences help young adults grow spiritually by allowing them to give themselves away in Christ-like service to others.

Topical Studies

Young adults will respond well to special studies of topics that speak to their needs and interest. Such studies might take place on a weeknight, or as the focus of a retreat. They can happen regularly or occasionally, but give variety and depth to a ministry based in Bible study. The purpose of these events is to let Scripture and the Christian world view speak to and inform young adult lives. The idea behind these kinds of events is to scratch where young adults itch, where they have a compelling interest and need. The end result is young adults who see the Bible as relevant to their own lives.

Exposure to Spiritual Leaders

Relational leaders will broker the opportunity for their young adults to meet a variety of spiritual leaders. The young adults can be introduced to visiting preachers, seminary professors, lecturers, foreign missionaries, denominational leaders and other influential Christians who can interact with them as friends. This can be done formally by attending a presentation, or informally by hosting the visitor for a casual conversation time with the group. Doing this allows the young adults access to otherwise unreachable leaders. It builds the group self-esteem and broadens their understanding. It also helps them connect with their broader Christian and denominational family.

Recreation and Fun Activities

No young adult ministry is complete without parties, fellowship, sports, games, and just clean fun. Fun builds family, which young adults crave. Fun breaks barriers and creates a climate for relationships to develop. Relational leaders work at providing plenty of opportunities for fun for their groups.

Games, sports and drama are three main fun-inducing tools at the leader's disposal. Games, both competitive and non-competitive can be use as crowd warmers, as ice breakers and get-acquainted activities. They can be passive or active, played in teams or by individuals around a table. At first, young adults may play the games grudgingly, just to please their older leaders. But is the game is really good, later on they can be caught playing it of their own accord.

Sports have a direct appeal to the energy they have in so much abundance, especially if they are co-ed. Formal and informal games of volleyball, basketball and softball are attractive to most young adults and as such provide the opportunity for Christians to include their non-christian friends in an unthreatening and inclusive experience. This will allow for a later sharing of the Gospel. Involvement in all-church teams and leagues allow young adults the chance to build cross-generational relationships.

Drama is a third great way to have fun. It can be done simply, as in easy role playing to illustrate a lesson point, or on ascending scales of difficulty. Drama teams performing pointed skits can enhance the Bible study and worship of the young adult group well as a ministry outreach tool. Those same teams can also be the spark plug groups to start or carry on church-wide drama efforts.

Planned Spontaneity

On of the issues of planning fun, however, is the tendency of young adults to be tentative in commitments to attend and be involved. There seems to be an almost universal trend to wait to the last minute to keep all the options open. Leaders need to recognize this, if only for self-preservation. The secret to avoiding a situation where leaders have spent a great deal of time in preparation only to have only one or two persons show up for a party planned for twenty is simple. Exercise planned spontaneity.

Planned spontaneity is easy. Leaders look ahead and choose dates for special events, things like movie nights, or pizza parties, or after-church meals. They schedule it on their calendars, and perhaps even mention the event in by announcements or in print. On the night before the event, or the Sunday morning of the event, phone or announce to the group that it is going to happen.

Everyone will likely have forgotten what was happening anyway and be surprised and pleased to do something "on the spur of the moment."

The purpose of planned spontaneity is to protect the leaders' mind and body. By announcing the event ahead of time you please those who do indeed plan ahead. By recruiting attendance at the last minute you fit into young adult life style and habit. Everyone wins with planned spontaneity.

Relational leaders understand the rhythm of young adult ministry

A common experience of young adult leaders is to have several periods (weeks, months, years, you pick) of success. Nothing seems to go wrong. Everything is in a growth mode. Then seemingly overnight, things fall apart. Bible study and event attendance drops. Faithful leaders disappear. The core group shrinks. You can no longer count on the ones you could.

Such disasters will cause you to question everything from your call to your aptitude for ministry. Those experiences shake your confidence and bring on anxiety and even despair. The bad news is that these kinds of things happen to young adult groups all too regularly. If they have not happened to you, just wait and they will. The good news is that ministry has a life-like rhythm. If you are faithful and consistent, things will pick up. If you wait long enough, the rhythm will begin again.

At its heart this rhythm is the transitory experience of the young adults themselves. Their life is in transition, and so is everything they touch. Dating couples marry and move to other classes. The semester at the local college changes and there is no strong new "crop" of folks. Work schedules change. A favored Sunday School teacher moves away. Somebody gets mad or miffed. The mega-church in town starts a concert series and no one else can compete. All these and other factors are at play in the ebb and flow of young adult ministry.

Route 6
Technique - A Variety of Methods

Every fisherman knows that to catch a certain kind of fish requires the right kind of bait. It needs to be or look like dinner for particular fish in that particular stream or pond. Fly fishermen can use some of their hand tied feather lures only on certain streams at certain times of the year. Use that fly on another river for another kind of fish and nothing happens. This situation holds true whether you fish for bass with glittery minnow-shaped lures deep in the pond, or for sailfish with mackerel. Fish will strike what they like.

Since Christian ministry is like fishing (fishers of men, and all that!), the same thing holds true: young adults will strike what they like. This is the starting premise of all young adult ministry. It is rooted in bringing the Gospel to bear on the needs, issues and values of young adults. These areas must always be the starting point.

Churches must use the right "hooks" to catch young adults for Christ, and they must have plenty of them in the water. As in fishing, ministry with young adults calls for a variety of methods, techniques used to fit the situations and need the needs.

Technique #1: Meet the needs and speak to the interests of young adults.

Young adults respond best to preaching, teaching, programs and ministry that meets their real and felt needs and which grasps and holds their interest.

When trying to reach an audience that ranges from the committed, but preoccupied, to the disinterested, to the hostile, it is important to remove as many barriers as possible. Appealing to what appeals to them, to what makes them "hungry", will attract their primary interest. It will also keep, and hold their attention when other things might not be quite as interesting.

Technique #2: Put young adults first and institutions second.

Church structures and organizations must serve the young adult; not the other way around.

Previous discussions affirm the Bible as the foundation for ministry, but young adults are the reason. We have ministry because young adults need it. They need the Gospel for salvation and life guidance. That is the "why" of this entire enterprise. Structures or programs do not exist for their own sakes, but for the Gospel's and young adults'. Everything must resonate with them and their needs. If we seek to perpetuate a program for its own sake, and at the expense of our young adults, we do a disservice.

Technique #3: Understand that because young adults are widely diverse individuals they learn in widely diverse ways.

People vary radically from one another. Young adults vary more so. Each is different and brings to relationships and learning situations their own set of unique features. Put simply, each person has his own preferred way of leaning. Some learn best by hearing and listening. Others learn best by seeing or reading. Still others really comprehend when they do or act. Some folks have to see, hear, feel, do and even tell to learn best.

Want to succeed in creating an environment where young adults and the truth of Scripture collide so that both win? Then teach with variety and enthusiasm.

A good place to start is by connecting with your young adults. Become a family by creating an atmosphere of caring and love. Give them opportunity to meet others and get acquainted. Have plenty of shared fun and serious experiences so they become friends. Speak and teach from your heart with sincerity and authenticity. Promote participation and interaction by drawing them out with loaded or directed questions. Foment discussion. Present a challenge. Cement your relationship, and show your authenticity by using lots of personal illustrations, stories and examples.

Today's young adults relate first to the story, then, maybe much later, to the truth or doctrine the story portrays. Narrative testimony appeals more to them than propositional apologetics. [2]

The power of story is the power to infuse the mind with imagery so that it can vicariously undergo the events, experiences and feelings that take place in the story. Story reaches not just the intellect. Story reaches to the most deeply buried part of the human personality, to the emotions, and even to that mysterious elusive part of us that we know only as the human soul. A powerful story tingles our spine, surprises us with laughter, melts us to tears, moves us to righteous anger, tugs at our heartstrings, rivets our psyche, involves our pneuma, refashions our worldview, colors and filters our perspective, renegotiates our belief structure, calls into questions our assumptions and ultimately leaves us a changed human being.[3]

Five sign posts give you some clue if your teaching and their learning are intersecting. First, ask yourself, "Am I stimulating them to learn?" "Do I appeal to their interests, or needs, or do I present them a problem or situation to be solved?" If you do that, you just might be teaching and they just might be learning.

Second, you should ask yourself about their involvement in the lesson. Do they ask questions, or, better yet, answer yours with enthusiasm? Do they discuss with each other, even sometimes to the point of friendly debate? If they do, the signs point to learning taking place.

The third signpost has to do with purpose. Does your teaching demonstrate purpose and a goal? Does it communicate the purpose for study, and does it lead the young adults to see and "buy in" to that purpose. If it does, they might actually be learning something.

The fourth question you should ask yourself is this: "Do I apply the truth of scripture to the lives my young adults are living? Am I making the application clearly and blatantly?" If you can answer in the affirmative, then learning is happening.

Finally, good teachers look at the signpost of assimilation. They must ask themselves if what they teach and apply is making the journey from the young adults' heads to their hearts to their hands and feet and mouths. Is the scripture truth being taken into their lives and put into practice? If it is, then they really are learning in the truest and best sense of that word.

Technique #4: Use one or more locations as a base for young adult ministry.

At, from, and with the local church

The first location from which ministry happens is the local church. This church decides to minister to young adults of all ages and life situations and sets about doing it. It includes young adults naturally in its Bible teaching program, and uses its facilities as a base for outreach and fellowship. The church is the base camp where young adults gather first before spreading out.

To make this ministry successful, we must be aware of some of its weaknesses. The first is the perennial problem of any church work: lack of leaders. Often, no one emerges to lead the young adult ministry, to be the teacher. If that is the case, perhaps other arrangements ought to be made. Perhaps recent high school graduates could stay in the youth department for one more year. Perhaps the church could enlist them as apprentice leaders and teachers in the youth or even children's area of the church's Bible study ministry. Whatever happens, the church must never give those young adults a legitimate "out" from church involvement. Do that, and they disappear for a long, long time.

Second, familiarity with a young adult ministry can be a problem. As the ministry exists for a period of time, the church may lose its initial excitement or interest in it as a special need. The ministry stands liable to the same kind of "take-it-for-granted-ness" that afflicts church ministries that do not keep their needs and stories fresh in the hearts of the people. One remedy for this is a subtle, but constant campaign on the part of both participants and leaders, to keep the hopes, needs and concerns before the church as a whole. They will publish regular articles or announcements in the church newsletter, or worship bulletin. They will publicize events and activities on a church-wide basis. Whenever they have opportunity, they will communicate the personal and corporate prayer needs of each young adult throughout the church family.

All a church needs do to have a church-based ministry, is to just do it. Ask God to raise up the right leaders. Enlist them, train them, and put them to work. Begin promising your youth group some great place for them after high school graduation, and follow through on that promise. Make young adult ministry as important and as well supported as any other church work. Be intentional. Make it happen.

On the college campus

A campus-based ministry takes place on a college campus and is aimed directly at the college student. The campus ministry may or may not relate to a local church. It might be the work of a particular denomination. Occasionally, ministry entrepreneurs will seek to start their own on-campus ministry and then seek the support of Christian individuals or churches for their work.

Often the campus ministry leader is a professional or full-time volunteer who will spend each day meeting with individual students for discipleship or planning. This leader will often give strong direction to the personal and spiritual lives of the students in the group, as well as to the events that the group plans.

Good campus ministry is evangelistic, boldly confronting the campus for Christ. Good campus ministry trains leaders. It holds them accountable to God and the group for the accomplishment of plans and projects. Good campus ministry focuses students beyond themselves to the greater world off campus, through mission, evangelism, and work projects, at home or even in foreign countries.

Campus ministry can be strong because of its focus on specific issues. It can be strong as the leaders spend valuable one-on-one time discipling others and as more mature student believers disciple less mature ones. It is strong as it helps students evaluate their education in light of Biblical values and mores, and as it brings academic disciplines under the judgment of Scripture. Its strength in its leaders, and the devotion they bring to their ministry. A campus ministry advances the Kingdom as it provides its participants with intense personal growth, and a built-in community at a time when these are most important.

There are some weaknesses, however. Student participants may develop a stronger loyalty to the campus ministry than to a local church. They often tend to focus their loyalty there because it has most adequately met their needs. It is a theological weakness, however, if the ministry forgets the scriptural primacy of the local church. There is often a lag time between graduation, moving into a career, and full involvement in a local church. Many times, the campus ministry will move its leadership from participant to "staff," thus postponing local church involvement.

Campus ministries are susceptible to at least one other major weakness, spiritual pride. Since they have full time leadership and well-defined strategies, it is easy for them to feel superior to the local church, which must be more diversified and less intense in its focus. This pride can lead to strained or broken relationships with church leaders. Such strain bleeds over into the attitudes of the students, and impacts their views of the church.

Campus ministries have and will continue to make contributions to the life of the church. Their product is mature believers, trained in leadership. Those leaders emerge with a Great Commission world view, broader than any regional or doctrinal parochialism. Campus ministry has inspired young adults to mission service, and dedicated social action. Most importantly, it historically nurtures young adults into receptivity to the great movements of God, movements that have impacted the entire church.

With a church ministry on campus
Churches can use campus ministry as a part of their intentional evangelism strategy. This can be done in a couple of ways. First, the church can sponsor an on-campus Christian club on a local college campus. One church can sponsor it alone, or in cooperation with other churches, or the denomination. The church doing this needs consistent, aggressive and responsible elected or hired leadership, as well as the cooperation of the college administration. Always work with and through the college administration.

Second, the church doing campus work can do so through a denominational agency. In many states the Southern Baptists, for instance, will sponsor campus ministries. Such campus groups are usually sponsored by Southern Baptist associations of churches and funded from a variety of sources that include the association and Cooperative Program funds from the state and national conventions.

With a new church-start
The newest approach to young adult ministry is a community based model of starting a church just for them. The beauty of this approach is that it appeals to the "adultness" young adults seek. It says plainly that someone considers them valuable and special enough to minister to directly. A young adult or "baby buster"

church will do the right things for young adults, speaking to their needs and issues with their own voice.

Leaders of a young adult church start will promote a spirit of fellowship and ministry that reflects the mindset of this generation. Its "atmosphere," or "ambiance" will be generation appropriate, and not be that of its parents. It will be relaxed and casual, using a variety of methods to communicate the gospel. Dieter Zander suggests that four 'R's' of ministry describe such a church: real, rousing, relevant, and relational. He says,

> *When you're real, you gain Busters' trust. When you are rousing, you gain their attention. When you are relevant, you speak their language. And when you're relational, you build bridges to the next generation. To previous generations these are important ingredients in ministry. To the Buster generation, these ingredients are essential. Without them you'll not engage the heart, mind, and soul of this new generation.*[4]

A young adult church will have plenty of music. It will reflect their styles and interests. This will be simple, mainly guitar music, with some drums and keyboards. Worship will be interactive and experiential. It will have a casual flavor, with more conversation. Drama and story-telling will play a great part of the services. Community-building will be a major goal of this kind of church.

Small groups for ministry, support, and Bible study will help this happen. Discipleship focuses outward. Everyone attending, believers and unbelievers alike, will be challenged to get their hands dirty in authentic servanthood through service projects to the poor, homeless and otherwise helpless people.

Preaching will be relational and invite interaction. The preacher will have a conversational style, and yet will be bold in the telling of the "hard" teachings of the Gospel about life-style and commitments and ethics. He will challenge his hearers to weigh his words for themselves, but will not let them escape without first seeking to get them to apply them. Application will be blatant and focused.

Evangelism will be a priority, but it will be an evangelism of process and relationship. This generation will be won to Christ slowly, gently and as a result of seeing Christ being genuinely lived out in a believer's life. It will not be won by rational thinking or by presentation of empirical evidence. [5]

The priesthood of the believer will be a very vital part of young adult church government. The church will function by team action and process. It will seek and develop leaders from among its own congregation more intensely and intentionally than ever before. Pastors will see themselves as equippers of lay leaders, and will seek others to train and disciple.[6]

Starting viable young adult churches is a process involving several ingredients. Yes, it is possible for one or more persons to go somewhere, rent a facility, make announcements and start a church. Whether this kind of church will last and prosper is another issue. Like all grand enterprises, these ministries take prayer, planning and preparation. They take both people and money. Like church starts of any kind, young adult churches will thrive best when started with the support of a visionary, more established church as its sponsor. It will grow as that church prays for it, and supports its as much as it can.

Technique #5: Always study the Bible first.

A quality young adult ministry studies the Bible for content and application. Application must be the key thrust. Learning Biblical knowledge for its own sake will no long appeal to the practical minded nature of today's young adults.

At church this is what the Sunday School does. Often a Bible study ministry for young adults is a Sunday School ministry, and exists as a regular and on-going part of the church's programming. For an established church, strengthening the Bible study ministry is the very first step to having a strong young adult work. If a church has a strong youth Sunday School, it follows that it needs a growing young adult Sunday School also. This can be a first strong step in breaking the cycle of dropping out of church after high school.

Using Sunday School as a primary approach has great value. First, it ties young adults to a needed foundation for living and salvation. Second, the Sunday School, through its regularity, and consistency, provides an on-going context for the connection and "family" young adults need. Third, it connects them with the Body of Christ in the world, the church. Fourth, it provides a legitimate "place" for young adults in the Church at a time when they are seeking such a place. Fifth, it provides the organization for aggressive, intentional outreach, ministry and evangelism.

The main concern of this approach is to study the Bible. The time and place are secondary. Times other than Sunday morning may be better for young adults. Weeknights or Saturday nights are options. Anytime anyone can gather anybody to study God's word is appropriate. A church using a strong Bible study approach may just schedule young adult studies at a variety of times and places.

The idea is to give as many people the opportunity to learn as possible at times when it is convenient for them.

This approach is not without its difficulties, problems that arise in the organization and method of Bible teaching, rather than with the Scriptures themselves. Rigidity or inflexibility will not work, and will turn young adults away. They may see Sunday School as too tied to an institution, and therefore suspect. Teachers may forget that the responsibility for the learning that takes place in class is more theirs than the young adults, and not be as well prepared as they should be. Teachers may only teach for content knowledge without making pertinent application, or they may not understand that there is more to teaching young adults than just giving a lecture. What ever happens, teachers must avoid being boring or irrelevant. Remember, being boring or irrelevant is a "kiss of death" with young adults.

We know that God's word is powerful, like a two-edged sword, and that it will not return to Him empty. We can teach young adults the Bible with faith, knowing that He will finish what he starts in their lives by the hearing and learning of the Gospel.

Technique #6: Use personal discipleship methods.

A discipleship-based ministry seeks to produce mature, growing Christian disciples whose aim is the deeper Christian life. Leaders in this kind of ministry involve participants in courses of study that focus on basic Christian disciplines, such as personal quiet times, scripture memorization, inductive Bible studies, journal keeping, sermon note taking and prayer. A major goal of this ministry is to help young adults internalize and apply the Scriptures to every aspect of their lives. Leaders spend much of their time in on-on-one counseling and mentoring. This approach calls for the participants to submit themselves in some degree to the authority of a spiritual director or advisor.

Leaders in discipleship ministries focus on a few young adults and aim to equip them to minister to others in the same way. Leaders seek to reproduce themselves in the lives of others. The end result of this work is dedicated, scripture-literate people with a strong sense of God's direction in their lives.

This model, a favorite of many campus ministries, does have some difficulties. First, it is personnel intensive, even more so than young adult work already is. It may be better suited for campus work than for the local church. A powerful discipleship-based ministry demands one or more full time ministers. Second, it produces devout, but "lop-sided" believers, folks who are good at introspection, but have an underdeveloped Christian world view. They also tend toward spiritual pride, and even a bit of arrogance when they compare themselves to other, less disciplined believers.

Technique #7: Provide opportunities for young adults to help other people.

While young adults understand the needs in overseas lands, they feel most powerful when they are dealing with needs in their own back yard. Ministry based groups focus on the "doing" of ministry, on the meeting of peoples' immediate and pressing needs. Groups with this focus spend their time planning, training for and carrying out various projects throughout the year. In the winter, they may serve at local homeless shelters or rescue missions. When spring comes they are out building homes along side other volunteers. Summer involves them in witnessing expeditions to Indian reservations or some foreign country. The fall has them working for voter registrations or literacy programs.

There is no doubt about the need for these ministries or the value they add to young adults. One concern is the "busyness" of too intense a program. This kind of program can get caught up in the details and the physical labor of it all to the extent of forgetting the spiritual aspects.

Technique #8: Build in plenty of time for fun and fellowship.

Fellowship-based ministry relies on social events, parties, outings, and plain good times to draw crowds and build commitment. Young adults need fun events which function as a means of meeting new people and finding that all important "connection." A church who provides fellowship opportunities for young adults will be at a good starting place for ministry. Key words for the success of these events are: rousing, well publicized, organized, needs-meeting and target group appropriate.

A ministry that is *only* fellowship based is, however, inadequate and shallow. Such a ministry will have great times, but grows very little. It already has lost sight of its reason for being, that of sharing the Gospel with young adults.

Route 7
Balance-A Considered Self-Control

Balance in Your Personal Life
Building character traits, developing a strategy and doing the work of the ministry are arduous tasks. It takes time, effort and energy to develop and fine tune them in your life. "Practice makes perfect" is the bottom line. Your ministry with young adults is the anvil on which the character traits are hammered out, and the

strategy fined tuned. The ministry is the place were lives are transformed.

The reality, however, is that the human mind, body and spirit can take only so much hammering and fine tuning. In spite of your working on these elements in your character you will eventually come to the end of your energy. People work is exhausting work. Young adults are "people" to the "nth" degree. There will be a time or times when you will feel weariness or exhaustion or burnout coming on. If you do not act quickly you will be in danger of entering into a "burnout zone." When, not if, that happens you will have no energy or even desire to continue your ministry. You will not ever want to see, hear or talk to anyone under thirty again.

When that time comes, and it will, there is something you can do. You can carefully, prayerful and with complete intentionality maintain an equilibrium as you live your life. Pay attention to this need for balance and burnout can be avoided, or if it comes, can be less devastating to your work.

Balance means staying on an even keel, and not going to extremes. It is maintaining an equilibrium in you life and ministry so that everything is running smoothly. While commitment to Christ must be total, the exercise of that commitment needs balance. The example is that of a marathon runner who paces himself, gains a steady speed so that he is able to finish well. This is what the author of Hebrews meant when he admonishes us to "run with endurance the race that is set before us" *(Hebrews 12:1)*. Seeking balance in ministry is to pace yourself in all areas.

Scripture teaches that there is an order of priority in the four main areas of family, work, play and ministry. To understand balance in your personal life means understanding and following the biblical order. This order comes directly from God's act of creation. The family was the first institution established after God created Adam and Eve *(Gen. 1:27-31, 2:18-25)*. Work was given them when God assigned them the task of cultivating and keeping the Garden of Eden *(Gen. 2:25)*. A good case can be made for play being next in the order. God rested, re-created, on the seventh day *(Gen. 2:1-3)*. It was only after the Fall that overt religious activity came into being. The purpose of the worship was to restore the order thrown off balance by rebellion. That balance was only fully restored when Christ came, and, conclusively, in his life, death and resurrection brought God and mankind back together again.

All four areas must be functioning correctly for a person's life to have balance. The issue is not everything having the same or equal amount of energy expended on its behalf. Balance has to do with giving each area the correct, but not necessarily, equal amount of time and energy. All four are vital to your physical, mental and spiritual health. Pay attention to each area of your life correctly and with the right amount of emphasis. If you will do this, you will achieve balance. This balance will empower you to function to your highest capacities. It will empower you to be the best servant of God you can be.

Balance in Your Ministry Life

The best young adult ministry has balance and equilibrium. It incorporates elements from each of the techniques we listed and is founded on a balanced personal life. Quality ministry will have the Bible as its basis and primary focus, for everything else springs from it. Spiritual maturity will be a desired outcome, and emphasize the development of the discipleship disciplines. Ministry and missions will happen as young adults obtain a Christian world view that begins at home and reaches out to the entire world.

Fellowship and family will be an outcome of ministry, service and study, as well as the cement that binds the group together and to the church. A balanced ministry incorporates fun and serious times, introspection and extroversion, loving God, loving self, and loving others.

Conclusion:

Unless we are Abraham, we usually do not start on a trip without knowing our destination. In the case of young adults, our quality ministry with them is a worthy destination. It is not easy to reach because getting there demands our travel on severely winding routes. To get there we must travel the route of the heart, with a sense of divine call.

We must take the high road of character, that causes a dedicated personal life. We must choose the bright paths of knowledge and wisdom for understanding and a strategic plan. Then, we must change into the fast lane of action, while at the same time keeping our load, fuel consumption and direction all in the best balance for travel. This is a busy journey, with a destination that is itself a highway with large numbers of companions.

[1] Mortimer J. Adler and Charles Van Doren, How to Read a Book: The Classic Guide to Intelligent Reading (New York: Simon and Schuster, 1972), pp. 3-15.
[2] Kevin Ford, Jesus for a New Generation, p.220-225.
[3] Kevin Ford, Jesus for a New Generation, p. 225. See also Leighton Ford, The Power of Story: Rediscovering the Oldest, Most Natural Way to Reach People for Christ (Colorado Springs: NavPress, 1994), p. 77.
[4] Celek and Zander. Inside the Soul of a New Generation, p. 108.
[5] Kevin Ford. Jesus for a New Generation, pp. 186-217.
[6] "alt.ministry@genX.forum", in NEXT from Leadership Network, vol. 2, No. 2, April 1996.

Section Five

Hazards on the Ministry Highway

"The Lord says, 'Clear the road! Get it ready for my people.'" Isaiah 57:14 (CEV)

When I travel, I like to know about potential road hazards. Do I need chains over the Grapevine? Is there construction on the 5 between Manteca and Modesto? How is the traffic flowing on the 405 South of LAX? This information helps me choose the routes to take, helps me avoid delays, and prepares my mind for those delays or detours I do have to take.

The same is true in ministry. If we know the hazards specific to young adult ministry ahead of time, we can plan to either avoid them or deal with them as they come. That knowledge makes it possible to have a safer, more fruitful journey. I have identified seven prominent "road hazzards" which you need to consider as you minister with young adults. These hazzards are not necessarily dangerous in themselves. Knowledge of these ministry features will help you navigate the road.

1. False Impressions

Church leaders sometime have the impression that young adults are like Martians with no connection with "real" people. The easy way out is to claim the differences are too much to breach, to give up on them. Most such impressions are false, because they are only impressions. Below are some common false-impressions and responses.

All those tattoos, earrings, nose rings, other body piercings, long hair and baggy clothes are signs of a Godless rebellion!
Perhaps they are. For some these things might mean defiance and rebellion. They are also a demonstration of how disdainful they are of their own bodies. If they have come to believe in their own lack of worth, it does not matter what they do to their bodies. Decoration can be permanent as well as temporary.

These things can also be symbols of their desire to belong to some group, any group of their peers. Tattoos or body piercing, for example, may be the actions of only one group or sub-culture of young adults. Researcher Ken Baugh lists six of many Generation X subcultures, each with its own unique style, dress, and attitudes: Slackers, Underground Xers, Urban Xers, Extreme Xers, Digital Xers, and Super Xers.[1] Each group is likely to have its own set of "rules" regarding dress, tattoos or piercing. It may or may not be something they do.

The only answer to this is to point ourselves in Jesus' direction and notice that he never hesitated to deal frankly, boldly and personally with fringe people. Look how he dealt with lepers and Samaritan women, not to mention Gentiles like us!

They are too smart for me to teach.
Actually, today's young adults are not smarter or dumber than any other person at this age. Do not confuse the reflected ramblings gained in a first year philosophy, sociology, history or science class with set-in-concrete life attitudes or opinions. These folks try on new ideas and concepts like we try on shoes when we go shopping.

Another factor is that as a leader of this group you are certainly more experienced in life than they, and have much to offer them. Also, it is likely, if you are like the workers we surveyed, you have as much or more formal education than many of your young adults will ever have.[2]

They do not want older adult friends.
This statement is patently untrue. They do want older adults as their friends. Every young adult I have related to as a friend has responded in kind. They are receptive to relationships with older people. What we have to understand, however, is that these must be relationships of equality, not of superiority/inferiority. Young adults understand full well the difference that age, education, and experience make, but would rather come to love and respect you first as a friend with whom they occasionally "hang." It is friendship that gives older adults the right to give advice and suggestions, to teach and admonish. One's position as a Sunday School teacher only gives a forum or platform for these kinds of relationship to begin. Begin, and they will continue if given half a chance.

They do not care about the church and God
This statement is only partially true. It is more correct to say that they do not care about a church that is irrelevant and unresponsive to their needs. They care about reality, about life, and about meaning. We know that God is real, alive and meaningful, and so do many of them. It is up to us, however, to demonstrate that the church is a place where genuine relationships happen because of a God who is real.

They want to stay in the youth group.
Young adults who have been active throughout high school in their youth groups naturally want to stay connected with those groups after they graduate, especially if they are staying in town.

This is natural, for the youth groups provided family and security for them. They have had great fun and spiritual experiences in those groups. Who would want to give that up?

It is important for church leaders to recognize that recent high school graduates need to have some kind of continuing relationship with the youth group. At the same time those graduates need a way to express themselves as growing young adults. Depending on your own circumstances you could 1) have a graduates' class attached loosely to the senior high class or department; 2) move young adults into their own class, but use them as sponsors for youth activities; 3) provide such a quality young adult-oriented ministry that they have no real desire to be attached to the youth group; 4) plan ahead enough that college-career ministry is an integral part of your youth ministry strategy, building in anticipation for moving on to the next age-group level throughout each year of the youth ministry.

2. Ministry in the Smaller Church

Smaller churches often feel they can do little to minister to young adults. Since most churches are about that size, nothing much gets done. On the other hand, if a church wants to do something, it can. If it has an attitude of openness to God, to finding out where He is already at work and going with him there, then something will happen.

The question is simple. What happens when those three high school seniors graduate? Will you place them in a "single" adult class with two single parents, and a divorced lady old enough to be their mother, or in the younger of the two regular adult classes? Will you just inadvertently "write them off" because they are going to disappear anyway? Or, will you take positive steps to preserve and keep them, even those three? Here are some suggestions:

Suggestion #1: *Start a New Young Adult Sunday School Class*

A small church may have only three high school graduates, or two, or one! What an opportunity! The experts tell us that new units grow faster than older ones, and that the ideal class size is around 10-15 with an enrollment of about twice that. A new class, with a core group of three, can be the growing point for any church. There are plenty of recent high school graduates "out there" for this class to have potential. There are three areas of potential. First, other recent graduates, friends of the core group who are not believers, but might be interested in joining the group. Second, the church can enlist Christian young adults who have left their home church but need and want involvement. Third, it can reassure the up-coming high school juniors and seniors that it does care about them. The church can help them understand that it expects them to stay involved after graduation.

There are several spots for a new class in the Sunday School organization. 1) This class could join with the high school class, or the high school juniors and seniors as a part of an Older Youth department. 2) The recent graduates could become elected leaders and helpers in the Sunday morning youth Bible Study, with special Bible study times for them held on Sunday evening or some other time during the week. 3) It could be set up as an entirely new College and Career Class with strong Bible study, fellowship and outreach.

Suggestion # 2: *Enlist a Sunday School Care Leader whose only job is to keep up with the Young Adults.*

Not every church can have a young adult ministry. Every church can minister to them. Since you are reading this, perhaps you should be the one to volunteer to be the contact person for this group. You can be the one to contact and encourage the young adults. They may be lax in their attendance, but they still need to know the church cares.

This approach has a couple of variations. First, the adult Sunday School class to which the high school graduates would be assigned takes responsibility for them. Yes, everyone else in that class is old enough to be their parents, or has nothing in common with them, but they still have the responsibility for them. Perhaps, they will not attend. Even if they do not, the key care leader and his group will need to "ride herd" on those young adults. This involves doing those things care groups normally do: phone calls, letters, cards, visits and just plain "pestering." Since young adults have a higher threshold to "pestering" than other adults, this will work. Young adults are high maintenance and need the attention, just to be convinced that folks do care.

3. Age Differences in Young Adults

The young adult years run roughly between 18 and 28. These are ten years of transition and change. As they pass through those transitions, they do so at different rates and order. It is possible to have a 25-year-old dealing with the same issues as an 18-year-old. However, each situation must be dealt with separately. Usually the group will take on the personality of the ages of the largest number of people. A younger group will attract younger people. An older group will attract older people. The emphasis the leader places will have impact too. If the leader focuses on retaining the recent graduates, there will always be a source of new class members, and the class age will remain young. If older young adults start coming, that presents a new opportunity to start a new class just for them.

4. Married Young Adults

Young adults see themselves as having a relatively open future. That future, whether far or near, often includes the possibility of marriage. That often happens. After all, it is the "way of all flesh," and a primary ingredient in God's plan for the earth. It is a great thing when young adults find their life mates from within the Christian faith. One of the major, but deliberately under-emphasized, purpose of a college-career group is to provide a safe place for young adults to meet, get acquainted and fall in love.

Two things can happen when young adults in the group fall in love, get engaged and eventually get married. First, they become totally caught up in each other to the exclusion of everything and nearly everyone else. The WEDDING becomes the end all and be all of their existence. For the leader of the group, it means that these two people attend only sporadically. If they were leaders, let them resign gracefully with blessings to focus on their wedding. Do not count on them as leaders.

Later on, as a married couple they may want to be active in college-career activities. Let them. As nature takes its course, and as other opportunities open up, the young-marrieds will naturally seek new arrangements of friendships and involvement. Once again, a church gains the opportunity for growth by starting or expanding a young marrieds' Sunday School class.

5. Single Young Adults with Children

A contemporary phenomenon is the young single parent: a young mother, or possibly a young father and child. Such an involvement is a real opportunity for ministry, for reclamation and for the expression of love and concern. Young adults love babies and small children and will generally be willing to help a young parent and include them in the larger group.

The problem of involving young parents and their children is the neediness level of that parent. They are inevitably and always struggling financially. Often they are living with their parents, and are under a variety of stresses that single young adults may not fully appreciate. They are often psychologically needy, demanding a great deal of attention and reassurance of their own self-worth.

Be wary of letting the needs of any one person become the reason of your group's existence. Keep the need and purpose of the group always in some kind of creative tension with those of that young parent. It is proper to include the child in some of the group's activities. It is also proper to insist that for some events it would be better for the child not to come. The leader can and should help solve any baby-sitting problems or financial issues.

6. Working with Church Staff

Lay people need to understand how to work effectively with salaried church staff. I believe that a reciprocity must happen. Lay people must join with the staffer in the accomplishment of the task the church is asking him or her to accomplish through participation, leadership and encouragement. In turn the staffer must empower lay people in ministry through vision building, training, encouragement and implementation.

If you as a lay person have a heart for young adult ministry, and the staff does not seem to, the first step is to be in much prayer, asking God to give that staffer or pastor a similar passion. It may be that the staffer wants to do something to reach young adults and retain your high school graduates, but has not had adequate, self-starting lay leadership with enough patience and endurance to make that ministry happen. Then, the lay person with the vision will put feet to their prayers, and action to their passion.

Young adult ministry will happen when church staff and lay leaders join in a common vision with a common passion and unified action.

7. Inter-Church Cooperation

In Merced, California the youth pastors of churches of many denominations meet for fellowship and prayer on a regular basis. A result of this relationship was the establishment of regular city-wide college-career rallies. These once-a-month events include recreation, mixers, music, prayer, a speaker, games, and food. The creators of these rallies realize that young adults love crowds and have worked to get those crowds for them. This large-group event gives church groups momentum and individuals the energy to go back to the smaller groups at church. The result in Merced is ten or twelve churches of various and no denominational affiliation meeting regularly to celebrate their common allegiance to Christ. They have a consistent attendance of forty or more college-career young adults. Churches in Merced seem to have caught a hint of the secret of success: that many can do tremendously more together than any one can do by themselves.

Two other ideas bear mentioning, with the fleshing out left to you.

A "Consortium Ministry"

Perhaps three or four churches of the same denomination could join together to hire one person as young adult and single adult minister. Supervision of this staffer would be done by a committee of representatives from participating churches, who in order to participate would pay an equitable portion of the staffer's salary and benefits. The staffer would have two main responsibilities: training local church workers with young adults, and direct ministry with the young adults of the participating churches. The staffer would maintain a circuit between participating churches, training leaders, assisting in the college-career Sunday School classes and promoting the ministry. Then on a specified night, all the young adults from the participating churches would gather for their regular rally, complete with lively music, food and solid Bible teaching.

A Referral Service

What about smaller churches deciding to be unselfish with their young adults and encouraging them to participate in the young adult ministry of a larger church of the same denomination in the same town? Doing this would not mean "abandoning" those people. Someone or some group in the home church would maintain regular contact. The home church could, with an understanding with the larger church, could continue to encourage their folks to come back to worship and other activities with the home church. This symbiotic relationship between churches calls for the larger church not to be selfish, and the smaller church not to be jealous. It would call for the leaders of both churches to put ministry above ego.

Conclusion

Scripture commands us to prepare the way of the Lord by making straight in the wilderness a highway for Him *(Isaiah 40:3)*. We can prepare in no better way than by removing all the obstacles that interfere with young adults from coming to Christ. We may have to do some planning. We may have to make some sacrifices. We may even have to give up some of our comfort and pet prejudices. If we do, if we take those things into consideration that will reach young adults, God will honor our work so that He gets the glory and whole carloads of new children!

[1] Ken Baugh. A Guide to Understanding Generation X Sub-Cultures (McLean, VA: Frontline Ministry Resources, 1996).
[2] Surveys of church work with college and career young adults were conducted in 1993 and in 1997. In both instances, 89% of those responding reported a college level or above education.

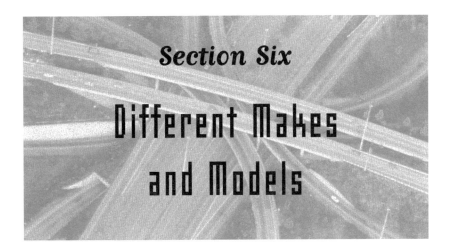

Section Six

Different Makes and Models

I recently purchased a new Buick Le Sabre. It is a great car with all the gadgets middle-aged guys like. Choosing the exact car was a simple process. I had decided early in the process what make and which model I wanted. I would have been very confused if I had not decided ahead of time.

The variety of makes and models of cars is astounding. There is a bewildering assortment from which to choose. There is a car for every preference in color, features and cost that people have.

Different folks with different needs and desires buy the car that best suits them. That is the way it is with churches too. While there are many similarities, there are also many differences. There are churches for every preference and need. Read how four churches, very much alike in many ways, yet remarkably different, reach out to and minister with young adults.

With churches, as with automobiles, there are different makes and models.

1. Suburban Intersections:

Young Adult Ministry at First Baptist, Poway
by Stan Gold

From 1990 to 1995 Stan and Karen Gold taught Young Adults in Sunday School at the First Baptist Church of Poway, a growing community in northern San Diego county. Dr. Ronald Shepard is the current pastor. First Baptist is a typical California Southern Baptist Church. It began in 1959 and has a membership around 600 with a Sunday School enrollment of 475. The Sunday School is the primary teaching and reaching arm of this church, though it has ministries for all ages and both genders. The work this church was doing came to our attention as a result of a series of young adult ministry focus groups the California Southern Baptist Convention held in 1993. What God did through that church and one dedicated couple for and with young adults is worth sharing. Stan shares his story with us:

Deciding to take the Trip
In 1990, my family and I joined the First Baptist Church of Poway. A Deacon and the Sunday School Director both approached us, asking about ministries we might like to have as members of Poway First Baptist. The church's ministry addressed all ages and special interests rather well except for young single and married adults 18-34. Those church leaders challenged my wife and me to start a College/Career Sunday School Class and promised full cooperation and support by the church leadership.

After extended prayer, it became clear that God was leading both the church and us to work with College/Career young adults. My wife and I elected to follow His leading.

We began the College/Career ministry in the Summer of 1990. Poway's Senior Pastor was gracious enough to give his complete support with the understanding that I would keep him informed of our activities and be subject to his periodic evaluation. This was a commitment I felt was essential for the existence of a healthy relationship between the young single adults and the church's spiritual leadership.

Packing Our Bags

Deciding to work with young adults was not a lightly made decision. Once we had decided, my wife and I began making plans to move ahead with our ministry. We took several kinds of action as we prepared. First, we prayed. We knew that no ministry would be effective without God's guidance and direction. Our prayers did not stop throughout the time we worked with this group.

Second, we did a survey of church membership rolls to discover those 18-24 year old church members no longer attending the church. We also looked over the then current church membership rolls to see if anyone 18-24 was attending or working in some other area of the church. When we gathered all that data we evaluated it to prepare a strategic action plan.

Only five names surfaced in our membership roll search, and only three of them looked very promising. To provide a simple first time contact with these folks I made up "cooler kits" to give to each one as a gift "out of the blue" from their church. These kits consisted of a six-pack of soft-drinks and a variety of non-perishables. Included in the kit was an invitation to our first College/Career beach outing.

Getting In and Starting Up

Our strategy was simple and basic, involving six steps:

1) We planned an event that was interesting, non-threatening and fun, which encouraged interaction within the group.

2) We contacted each prospect from our survey well in advance of the event and used the event to introduce ourselves and the newly created College/Career ministry.

3) We carefully tried to discover if the person we were contacting was interested in helping with the event. Some young adults are "Doers" while many are not. We knew it was important to be non-threatening yet encouraging at the same time.

4) We were looking for leaders, so we noticed those who were willing to volunteer their services and identified them as candidates for leadership. We did this because we believe leadership is what makes or breaks any ministry especially that with College/Career young adults.

5) We took stock of our spiritual arsenal and made a plan of attack. We knew that the start-up event would provide a great opportunity to explore young adults' opinions, as well as test the waters of their receptivity. Finding out what they thought allowed us to make any necessary minor adjustments.

6) Our regular Sunday School class offered topical Bible study each Sunday Morning. We studied current issues relating to young adults since we felt it was always a safe approach to begin. Making certain that the material is current, targeted and appropriate for young adults is vital to the success of any College/Career ministry.

Five people received invitations and five people came. It was the start of a wonderful ministry blessed by God. The College/Career ministry grew to 12 people the first six months and increased to 20 within the year. The ministry developed around a one hour intense Bible study each Sunday morning that focused on young adult issues and needs. The book of James proved to be a valuable starting point. It is extremely practical for young adults when the world and its stumbling blocks seem to get in the way of a nurturing relationship with God.

Fuel for the Journey

We knew that to be successful as leaders we needed to fuel the ministry correctly. That fuel had to be very compatible with the young adults, and certainly able to have high octane when we needed it. We found that because we were older and could have been seen as too much "the parent," a spirit of servant leadership worked best. Our young adults responded to our proactive, yet loving approach. They saw us as friends, but also as leaders who wanted to serve them and lead them to a closer relationship with Christ.

Our group was fueled by the fact that we sought to match their personal spiritual gifts with tasks that complimented those gifts. This resulted in more efficient and effective individual and group ministry. Motivating an individual in an area where he is most gifted is always rewarding to both the individual and the group.

We designed special events and activities to address the exclusive needs of both genders. We had "girls' nights out," women's Bible studies and the like for the women, and sports events, men's Bible studies and "guy-only" outings for the men.

We designed specific inreach and outreach ministries to nurture our existing ministry while reaching out to surrounding communities in fulfillment of Matthew 28:19-20.

We encouraged and enlisted individuals to look for and carry out their own personal missions' ministry. This helped enlighten them of the need for both home missions and foreign missions projects. We involved interested participants in the planning process of events, activities, retreats, workshops and leadership training.

Since many young adults like to play music, and all young adults like music, we developed a contemporary music ministry. Our purpose was two-fold: we wanted to involve as many of our young adults as possible, while at the same time providing a comfortable worship format for their non-Christian friends.

Because we wanted the young adults to feel a part of the larger church family, we encouraged their involvement in church ministries and weekly worship services. We also worked to involve them in the church's governmental structure whenever the opportunities presented themselves.

Finding the Drivers

Leaders should raise up other leaders. To do that in a group takes careful consideration. Knowing the people you ask to work along side of you is key to making wise leadership decisions. We had a vested interest in these people. It was important that they sensed our authenticity when we told them how much we really did care.

When our group reached a regular attendance of twenty, it was time to develop a "Planning Team." Seven core people prayed about becoming actively involved in such a leadership team. They gave me their answers within a week. God went to work and spoke to each of the seven in a very personal way. Every person responded with a positive commitment. Their primary task was to develop a calendar of activities and events for the entire year.

As the group continued to grow, it became evident that our need for a "Ministry Team" was genuine. It was time to step up our efforts in the area of spiritual maturity. Inreach and outreach activities became the next step in our development. Seven additional individuals were approached in much the same way as the "Planning Team" leaders. All seven responded positively. However, they did not all respond without reservation. This commitment would mean for them to tread uncharted waters and that was of concern to those who were still relying on self to get them through their problems. Although it was a little rocky at first, the "Ministry Team" began to work out the wrinkles and look to God for their primary source of direction.

Our outreach to the community expanded. Visitation became standard practice. We planned and carried out mission projects locally and south to Tijuana, Mexico. "Care Nights" designed to reach out to our "away" students on campuses outside the San Diego area also became part of our program. There was also a "Sponsor" program put into effect to greet new attendees to the class. The "Sponsor" would introduce the guest to various members in the class, update them on upcoming events and activities, and arrange to meet with them for coffee or a soft-drink sometime during the week. This relationship would continue for approximately a month or until the individual felt comfortably "plugged-in" with the group. The program proved quite successful.

A Mountain Destination

In 1991, I encouraged the Planning Team to consider planning an annual retreat for our college/career ministry. They agreed on having a 1991 Summer retreat at Palomar Mountain. I was admittedly a little disappointed with the small turnout of 8 young adults, but it was a start. The Planning Team received firsthand experience on ways to improve future retreats.

The success of the summer retreat motivated the Planning Team to plan a second retreat during the following winter. In January 1992, they had scheduled a retreat called Big Bear '92. The theme was "Prayer is Critical." This event drew twenty young adults to Big Bear and ignited a growing interest. The Big Bear experience was so dynamic that those in attendance were brought to their knees in tearful prayer. It was an incredible encounter with God.

We continued to have these two retreats a year for several years. Palomar '92 (the summer retreat) drew a group of 22, Big Bear '93 drew a group of 33, Palomar '93 drew 35, and Big Bear '94 drew a record group of 43. In 1995 we worked with the College and Singles Ministries Department of the California Southern Baptist Convention to expand our single-church winter retreat to become a regional event for young adults from many churches. Big Bear '95 drew 164 young adults from 11 churches. By 1997 the retreat had an attendance of 285 young adults from 25 churches and a local Christian college. The 1998 retreat drew 393!

Collecting the Passengers

By summer, 1992 the group had grown to approximately 30. As of spring, 1994 our enrollment exceeded over 50 and our 'away'(those college students who are away at college) roster was carrying an additional 15. Our college/career ministry represented 15% of the total Sunday School enrollment.

Expanding the Ministry

It has been my pleasure to nurture young adults and experience the fruit of my labors at Poway First Baptist. Several have felt God's call on their lives and are responding to that call. One young man is preparing to be a Youth Pastor; another desires to work with young adults; another young man is pursuing a call in the area of music. Several of our College/Career young adults have gone on to attend California Baptist College, Baylor University, Southwestern Seminary, Bethel Seminary and Golden Gate Baptist Theological Seminary.

The list is of young adults who are growing as disciples of Jesus is almost endless. I thank God for that.

Moving On

As I look at the work of God among College/Career young adults in Poway from 1990 to 1995, I see how God worked through my wife and me. He allowed us to think strategically, to enlist and develop leaders, and to involve our young adults in the full life of our church. He has allowed us to see the fruit of our work and encouraged us to continue. At this writing we are in new ministry areas, but God is still directing our passion for College/Career young adults. Our encouragement to you is this: nurture and send your College/Career young adults. It is God's way of blessing you beyond your greatest expectations.

Editor's Update

A later report on the young adult ministry at Poway shows the cyclical nature of that work. The pastor reports:
We are seeing a similar repeat of this story with a new couple. In the past seven years we are now in our third cycle with the third couple, enjoying the same fruit. Each of the couples are very different from each other, each coming to a similar situation. We have so far not yet successfully transitioned from the "planting" couple to the next level of leadership. Starting over with a base group of about six, we are now averaging twenty in Sunday School after 7 months.[1]

---

[1] Quoted from Pastor Ron Shepherd in a letter dated September 25, 1997.

2. Reversing the Trend

Young Adult Ministry at Concord Korean Baptist Church
by Tony Lee

Korean churches are faced with a unique cultural dilemma. They are composed of people living in two worlds: that of their eastern cultural and ethnic mileu, and that of western, American life-styles and culture. This article describes the situation, and tells how one church is striving to maintain a balance between cultures in terms they can understand.

Concord Korean Baptist Church of Martinez, California is a 632 member Korean-speaking congregation. Its founder and current pastor in 1998 is Dr. David Gill. One of its ministries is its English language department led by Rev. Tony Lee, a recent graduate of Golden Gate Theological Seminary.

In the August 1996, issue of *Christianity Today*, there appeared an article, *Silent Exodus*, which examined why a vast number of second generation Korean-Americans are wandering away from the first generation Korean churches, leaving their faith community behind.[1]   Although this article was not the foremost of its kind, it helped gain national attention among Asian-American Christian leaders, especially in reference to Korean-American churches. As the Korean-American population rapidly reaches its "major-minority" status among the Christians in the United States, the "Silent Exodus" has become a resounding alarm, leaving behind resonant echoes in first generation Korean churches.

The "Silent Exodus" is just a beginning. Second generation Korean-American young adults face a lack of English ministries within the Korean language church. In addition, they also find cultural barriers in assimilating into an English-speaking Caucasian congregation. This is an exodus without a future.

Unless this trend can be reversed with urgency, there will be a time of exile and spiritual decline among Korean-American churches. Mere optimism that the next generation Korean-Americans will eventually return to church life is nothing more than apathy disguised in sheep's clothing. Next generation churches must develop intentional and strategic plans, immersed in prayer. The *"If we build it; they will come"* approach in doing next generation ministry will face empty results. It lacks vision and purpose. For instance, the exodus of the Israelites came with a vision for a purpose: Moses encountered God in front of the burning bush to free His people from bondage to worship God. Sadly, the "Silent Exodus" is without vision or leadership.

Since the mid 1960's, a huge surge of Asian immigration to the United States provided fertile soil for a population explosion among Asian-American communities. According to the Federal Census Bureau report, Asian immigrants have become the nation's fastest growing group, which will reach more than 13 million by 2005. More significantly, as of January 1994, after a generation of immigration, the Korean population in the United States has reached over 1.5 million and it will continue to multiply at a significant rate with the second generation Korean-Americans.[2]

Not much more than two centuries ago, Korea, "The Hermit Nation," had absolutely zero significance among the Christian community. But now almost thirty percent of the 48 million people in Korea embrace Christianity.[3] In 1993, at least eight of the world's twenty largest churches were found in Korea. Consequently, similar growth patterns can be found in immigrant first generation Korean-language churches across the United States. There are now more than 2,000 Korean churches in the United States, more than 100 of which are in the San Francisco Bay Area.

Then, why are so many second generation Korean-American ministries struggling rather than thriving? Although there are some recent studies that explain possible "whys," they do not provide "how tos" for reversing the trend. The real issue is <u>how</u> we are going to resolve the leadership vacuum for the second generation ministries, not <u>why</u>. Furthermore, the question that should be asked is not "why are Korean-American twenty-somethings leaving the first generation churches?" Instead, we should be asking, "how are we going to reach them?"

Using experiences and examples from the current ministries at Concord Korean Baptist Church, in addition to insight from within a Korean-American standpoint, I will attempt to address the present models and needs of Korean-American ministry, from a personal perspective.

"A Church Within A Church" - The Building of the Temple

There are at least two models for starting a second generation ministry which are being implemented: establishing a "church-within-a-church" or planting independent churches. Currently, many first generation Korean churches respond to the exodus by providing English language programs to reach the second generation young adults. A main concern for the first generation church members is that too many of their children, after graduating from high school, are wandering away from their Christian heritage. More recently, some of the first generation church pastors have gone further into developing autonomous ministries for the second generation, providing necessary financial support to begin a new church model for the Korean-American churches, a "church-within-a-church."

In this conceptual model, the second generation congregation is recognized as an autonomous body within the existing church. To promote the unity of the church, the English-ministry pastor works closely together with the senior pastor. However, the English-ministry pastor has freedom and flexibility to develop his own vision, purpose, budget, and implement necessary ministry plans, instead of receiving direction from the senior pastor.

During my final year of seminary, I received an invitation to serve as the English Ministry Pastor at Concord Korean Baptist Church. Because my previous ministry experiences as a youth pastor in Korean churches ended in frustration, I was cautious and hesitant in accepting the responsibility. During the interview, I openly shared my fears as well as my vision for the second generation ministry with the senior pastor, David Gill (a first generation Korean pastor who now serves as my mentor). We both expressed our concerns for the growing needs of the next generation ministry. At the same time, even though the English ministry at CKBC would have autonomy, he wanted to ensure that I would not cause a rift between the two congregations. Too many other first and second generation Korean pastors have failed in working productively in harmony, so he was careful in discussing his desire in protecting the unity of the body. Pastor Gill has invested 20 years of his life in this church, and wanted to continue to see its effectiveness in future generations.

Developing a healthy relationship between first and second generation church leaders is not always an easy task. In many instances, conflicts between the first generation pastor and the second generation pastor are not redemptively resolved. Consequently, distrust, anger, bitterness and resentment often erupts between them. As a result, some second generation ministries split away from the first generation church, leaving behind emotional anguish among the church leaders and members as well. Too often, blame is passed between the two generations while the exodus continues.

I joined the pastoral staff at CKBC as the English Ministry Pastor in September 1996, with a primary goal of building a healthy relationship between the Korean and English congregations. Both of us are committed to establishing a team based on respect and trust. Of course, we have our differences in personality, ideas, spiritual gifts and leadership styles, yet we are learning to appreciate and value each other's strengths as well as weaknesses. We both agree that trust is not given. Rather, it is achieved through mutual submission *(Ephesians 5:21)*. Both of us agree to work together in cooperation with the commitment to keep the unity of the church, and developing a "church-within a church" model. We meet weekly to update each other on what God's doing in our ministries. I appreciate listening to Pastor Gill's wisdom, and drawing from his experience. God's hand is evident through this time of sharing and insight into the workings of each other's responsibilities.

A few of the second generation leaders have turned to the church plant model. They have chosen to seek a totally new beginning. Although it is extremely difficult without support, it is a price some are willing to pay to have total control and freedom to guide

their congregation.
Generation Next Ministry - "Here Am I, Lord, Send Me" to the
College Campus

Through a contact person whom I knew when I was his youth
pastor, last year my wife and I were invited to meet with a group
of twelve U.C. Berkeley students. Since most of them were seniors, they were on the verge of graduating from school. During
our first meeting, they openly shared about how most of them
did not have a relationship with God yet they wanted to find out
what it meant to be a Christian. Although prior to this event, my
wife and I were praying for an opportunity to reach out to college
students, we had no idea that God would answer our prayer in
this way, through this group.

Each week, we crammed together in a small apartment somewhere near the campus for fellowship, prayer and the study of
God's Word. During our Friday meetings, the students expressed
their doubts and fears about God. They knew about God; they
felt, yet they did not know God. Some demanded physical proof,
while some cautiously listened. I introduced the group to *Experiencing God* by Henry Blackaby. As I shared about God's grace
and how He demonstrated His power in our lives, the students
opened up and responded. One by one, God revealed himself to
them. The students came and shared about how God answered
their prayers. Together, we experienced God first hand. We boldly
asked God to hear our needs, and our prayers were answered.
They searched for the Truth, and the Truth found them.

A year later, as I stood in the middle of Sproul Plaza (University of
California, Berkeley campus), thousands of bodies swept by me
leaving only traces of emptiness around me. In their hard faces,
I was able to see through their hollow shells, to the inner dark-

ness, hiding themselves from the true presence of God. Isolated
in their walk, they hurried through the campus to seek the empty
knowledge which could only fill their minds and yet not touch
their souls. God was showing me a vision of the God-sized harvest here. A deep sadness flowed inside of me and I called to God,
"Here am I, Lord. Send Me." From that prayer was birthed a
college campus ministry based at our church, which is a vital link
for reaching the next generation of young adults.

Almost 40 percent of the total student body at U.C. Berkeley are
Asian-Americans. These students are seeking for an identity
through establishment of meaningful relationships with others.
They are eager to explore new friendships in new found freedom.
Sexual promiscuity among Asian-American college students is
much more common than in adolescence. Many newly-arriving
students turn to sorority and fraternity life to satisfy their need
for friendship. While their curiosity in searching for the meaning
of life invades their minds, the thirst for spiritual emptiness fills
their hearts. They hunger for authentic friendship and a true
sense of belonging.

Following Jesus' lifestyle as a model for reaching college students
for Christian living involves building a relational ministry. Jesus
spent much time eating with his disciples, discussing heavenly
knowledge in earthly conversation and dialogue. He taught God's
truth while eating with them around a common table. Many of
these events seemed causal and ordinary, yet they were divine,
relationship building, life-changing encounters through which
the disciples were being challenged with spiritual issues. Jesus'
interaction with them reinforced the Biblical teachings of discipleship, evangelism, fellowship and worship. The disciples not
only found truth, but also found the truth in a community.

It is clearly evident that this generation seeks truth in experiential encounters. They are not looking for a four-point intellectual presentation of the gospel outline. Instead, they are searching for spiritual truth in an authentic environment. Many reject traditional methods and ideals. Rather, they embrace tolerance of all values, yet they often lack the commitment to carry out their beliefs. In my experience, the communication of the message must be relevant: poetic rather than prose, storytelling rather than lecture. It needs to touch the heart. They need to feel the message, experience for themselves the power.

Another answered prayer for our college campus ministry at Berkeley was the student leaders who serve as our contacts. In a public university setting, student-led religious organizations (including Christian fellowship) are welcomed and encouraged. On the contrary, without student affiliation, religious groups have restricted access to the campus. Due to the graduation of the original group, we had few options available to us, but God has brought two Berkeley students and a seminary student volunteer who are committed to serving. With the help of our student leaders, we were able to constitute our campus ministry under the name, *Generation Next Ministry*.

Also, as we were praying for this new campus ministry, I received an unexpected blessing. Just three weeks prior to our first meeting on campus, a letter arrived from a former member of our original *Experiencing God* discipleship group, along with a check for $800.00. He had just landed a good job working in Silicon Valley and given this gift without knowing that he had funded the beginning of this campus work. I was speechless at God's timing.

We now meet weekly on campus. We are distributing flyers and starting a web page to promote the *Generation Next Ministry* to Berkeley students. We created a campus e-mail account to maintain contact with new prospects. Sitting around in a circle each week, I feel the presence of God. He is working in the lives of people around me. I silently rejoice that He heard my prayer for His harvest.

The Coming Harvest

There is a population explosion among second generation Asian-Americans, yet there are neither adequate facilities, nor leadership to accommodate this growing need. For example, in Contra Costa County, where our church is located, the Asian-American population represents the largest minority ethnic group. The mission fields of East-Asia have moved to the backyard of the San Francisco Bay Area. Many second generation Asian-Americans, however, encounter great difficulty assimilating into an English-speaking Caucasian congregation, feeling out of place and isolated.

Recently, I met with the third generation Japanese-American senior pastor of the Lord's Gate Ministry in Oakland, California. He came to the East Bay Area 12 years ago with a vision that God would establish an Asian-American church. His work grew out of the "Church Within A Church" model. When he first came to the church, it was predominantly a first and second generation Japanese-language congregation. Now the Lord's Gate is a vibrant ministry where more than 50 percent of his membership is comprised of Chinese-Americans. As I dialogued with him, I realized that although there are no proven models for Korean-American ministries, we can learn from other Asian-American churches who have begun a similar task. They can serve as resources and examples. I became hopeful for the future of my calling to serve in the Bay Area.

Only a year has passed since my wife and I came to Concord Korean Baptist Church, and we are witnessing God's vision through the lives of people. Our ministry is becoming a vital and active body of Christ. We embrace the diversity of people through various worship styles, affinity groups and fellowship activities. God has also brought more new members who are of non-Korean American backgrounds. We are no longer just a Korean church; we are truly becoming a multi-cultural and multi-generational church. We are building a bridge to link between three generations: the generation who has gone before us and the generation who will go beyond. Consistency and longevity are key elements in developing an effective young adult ministry. Strategic planning is futile without perseverance. Planting seeds will yield in crops after a great deal labor and the passing of time.

[1] Helen Lee, "Silent Exodus: Can the East Asian Church in American Reverse the Flight of Its Next Generation?" *Christianity Today,* August 12, 1996, 50-53.
[2] Dan Moon. The Growth and Future of the Korean Southern Baptist Churches in North America, Seoul: Paul Publishing Company, 1996.
[3] Ron Wilson, "Beyond M.A.S.H.: the Korean Church Grows in the Dark," *East Asia's Millions*, Spring 1994, 8.

3. Crossing Our Cultural Borders

Young Adult Ministry at Primera Iglesia Bautista del Sur
By David and Lilian Lechuga

Primera Iglesia Bautista del Sur is a Spanish language congregation of around 600, with a Sunday School enrollment of 455. Located in San Francisco, it is one of the leading Hispanic congregations in California. Dr. James Page was pastor during the time covered by this article.

David and Lilian Lechuga, are members of Primera. David serves on the worship team and as a Youth Counselor at Primera, as well as Sound Technician at Iglesia Bautista Hispana de Half Moon Bay (a church mission of Primera). Lilian is the Youth Sunday School Teacher and a Youth Counselor at Primera, as well as pianist at Iglesia Bautista Hispana. They both serve on the Jenness Park Hispanic Camp Committee of the Confraternidad de las Iglesias Hispanas de California.

They shared the writing of this article. Lilian wrote about the Spanish Young Adult ministry using interviews she conducted with some of the group leaders. Quotes in this section have been translated into English. David wrote about his experience with the English Young Adult ministry and also interviewed former members of the group for his background information.

Lilian writes about Spanish Language Young Adults
The Spanish Young Adult Ministry at Primera is organized around a planning group called the "Directiva" or a Directorate. It consists of a Director, Vice President, Secretary, Treasurer, and the

worship team, made up of three females and five males. The Directorate meets once a quarter for planning a calendar of events for each of the following three months. This form of planning contributes to the success of the group as a whole: "When things are done at the last minute, they don't work out. Everything should be done to reflect God's excellence, since He deserves only the best."

It is then the responsibility of the Directorate to promote upcoming activities and Bible studies, always with two to three weeks notice to the group. These announcements are given at the weekly Bible studies on Saturdays at 7 p.m. The group knows what to expect since the Saturday night program is always the same. One of their leaders has stated that "there is much coordination with the Directorate and the Young Adult group. We consult with the group to find out if they like the ideas, if they think it will work, and if they will collaborate. You see the unity and they know what will happen. The group decides."

They begin the evening with a Bible reading, followed by prayer. Then the worship team steps up to lead in songs. Next, the person giving the lesson has predetermined if games will be played before or after the study. There is constant communication in the previous weeks between the Directorate and the study leader. The Young Adults do not have a permanent Young Adult Leader other than those leaders who make up the Directorate. They draw qualified speakers from within their own group, the church, or invite outside pastors and ministers. They feel the Directorate approach to the Ministry is working well.

Finally, they take a collection. They keep the receipts for use within their group. There is always one or two that don't have money when they go out to eat, and in this way they can provide for them. They end in prayer and decide where they want to eat so they can continue talking and getting to know each other before they go home for the night.

Once in a while, the group also sets aside some evenings for self-help-type classes. Instead of a detailed Bible study, they have a short devotional and complement it with a short course such as, "How to do your taxes," "Using a Computer," or any other subject of interest to the group members. Of course, the Directorate screens the speaker before hand to be aware of what will be presented to the group.

Currently, the group's age range is 19 to 38. They do not target any specific age, instead they open the door to anyone who wants to attend: "We don't want to leave anyone out, since most of the people we get are feeling lonely." This could be attributed to the fact that many young adults leave their homeland (in Mexico, Central or South America) to come to the States alone to find employment and send money back home. Another reason for their loneliness may be due to their newfound faith in Christ, since a majority of Latin Americans come from a Catholic background.

The group acts like a family and brotherhood to that soul that longs for support. Here, they can find it in an environment with people their own age, who speak the same language. 1993 and 1994 were difficult years. However, since 1995, the group has been very stable. This is due to its leadership: "The Directorate has helped a lot in that they have a personal relationship with God that we can all see." This was also the year that their new identity was born. They would no longer be called "Spanish Young Adults" (Jovenes Adultos en Español), rather they gave themselves the name of "Obreros de la Viña" or "Workers of the Vineyard." This gave the group something to live up to.

Doryss has been with the group for one year. She has seen the group grow from 15 to approximately 35 that meet regularly. "When I began, we were 15, the other 20 young adults we obtained with much work," she says. This has been possible with the cooperation of the entire group through phone calls and personal visits. The latter has been a successful project that they have focused on lately; they make personal visits to those young adults that have been away for a while and try to bring them back to the flock.

Another recent project that has been a success is a night of fellowship with other churches. During this event, hosted by Primera Iglesia Bautista del Sur, Spanish young adults from nine different Bay Area churches gathered to hear preaching by Santiago Morales. Thirty-five young people received Christ as Lord and Savior three of those joined Obreros de la Viña. The rest were left in the hands of their respective churches as the Primera Directorate urged them to do follow-up on these new souls.

Although the group has continued to grow, there is something that hasn't worked. All day events on Saturday have a low turnout. Most of the young adults have Saturday jobs that require eight hours of their day. Consequently, they cannot take a day off, which leaves a very small group for all-day trips or activities. In regards to future plans, the Directorate hopes to implement events that involve the church as a whole, and to have more impact on the surrounding community by visiting children's hospitals, jails and just letting people know, "Hey, we're here."

David writes about the English Language Young Adults
In 1994 our English Young Adult group was flourishing with about twenty active people. We were all bilingual except two or three that only spoke English. We seemed to always have some outing

or trip to go to, even if it was only to catch the latest movie and a burger. Every Wednesday and Saturday night we had Bible studies and every Sunday after service we had Sunday School. Our fellowship was great.

There were two trips that we especially looked forward to every year—our trip to Jenness Park in September, and our snow-spiritual retreat in February to North Lake Tahoe. We talked and laughed about each trip for months afterwards, recalling the fond and not-so-fond memories. Of course, I don't have as many memories as the other members that have been at Primera longer. Still the few memories that I do have are enough to make me wish and long for those days again.

Then something started to happen, changes that at first were too subtle to notice. Cliques appeared within the group. Gossip and back-stabbing started to divide the group. Maybe we spent too much time together, and not enough time in God's word. Our Wednesday and Saturday night studies started to thin out. People began showing up only when there was some special activity going on. There was a lot of arguing within the group.

Whenever the members were asked why they did not come anymore, they simply said, "Oh, because so and so is there." We no longer went out, or called each other just to see how we were doing. During one year's time we had four couples get married. This added some strain on our already small group. Strain due to the new responsibilities of being newlyweds and for some, being new parents. This strain only helped kill our already dying group. Last year our annual snow trip had to be canceled because of either lack of funds or lack of interest. The Young Adults were crumbling and we didn't know what to do.

At one point, my wife and I tried to organize and head the English Young Adult Ministry. We would hold meetings at our apartment every other Saturday night with invited speakers to head the studies. The first month we had food and soft drinks for those who came. Which is why I think we had such a good turn out. But the expenses started to get too high for us to handle on our own. So one night we asked the group to consider any financial help with the food so that we could continue providing it. That night they all agreed to help with something. That was also the last night with a good attendance.

In no time at all, only three or four people had any interest in the studies. As usual, it was what I call the "core group"—the group that always seems to be involved with any planning or volunteering. It was too much of a disappointment for me to handle. I thought that *I* could bring the group back together again. I was wrong.

I made the mistake of placing more importance in the *number* of people that showed up instead of those few that were there. I wanted to have a large group, so when only a few people showed up, I would get upset. Those that were there felt unimportant and unwanted because of my behavior. In my haste I forgot one huge and important detail: God. I never stopped to think about what *God* wanted or what He had planned for our Young Adults. All I was concerned about was what I wanted the Young Adults to be like. Things don't work that way. There is no way that one can go against God's will and expect to win.

"Why Can't They Pull Together?"
Since ours is a bilingual church, the question might well be asked: "Why the division between Spanish and English speaking young adults?" "Why can't they just pull together?" "Why can't they just get along?" Well, I asked myself those very same questions.

As far as I can remember there has been very little contact between the two groups. What I mean by this is that although we
see and greet each other on Sundays, we do not spend any time
together as Primera's Young Adults. We do not have Sunday
School or Sunday Service together. We do not visit each other or
even call to see how we are doing. There are several major reasons for this separation.

The most obvious and troublesome reason is the language bar-
rier. Some of our English speaking members may not know Spanish well enough to learn in that language. The ones that do know
Spanish may or may not be fluent enough to feel comfortable
using it very much. Even within the Spanish language itself, there
are many differences that are significant enough to cause ripples
within the group. There are certain words that in one country
might have a harmless meaning and in another country that same
word might be an insult or just a vulgar word. This could be very
embarrassing for the teacher or person that uses it unknowingly.

This language difference is enough to make someone uncomfortable in class were we to unite the classes. I tried to attend the
Spanish Sunday School class when I first arrived at Primera. I
had a very hard time adapting to the strict environment and the
language change. Even though I speak Spanish fluently, there
are a lot of words the meaning of which I have yet to master. By
the time I understood what the teacher had said, the class had
moved on. So I was constantly trying to catch up.

The same problem would arise if the Spanish young adults were
to come to our classes. They would have a hard time trying to
understand the lesson itself. Making the study bilingual would
either offer too little information for the amount of time allowed
(1 hour), or the study itself would run late.

Secondly, there is a big difference between how the English and Spanish Sunday Schools are conducted. In the English Sunday School the atmophere is much more relaxed. This is in part a reflection of the relaxed environment in most American schools. There seems to be more tolerance for jokes and kidding around.

In the Spanish Sunday School there is more of a traditional teacher/student environment. There is always the opportunity to ask the occasional question or say the occasional comment. The rest of the time, the classes are much more formal. It seems this is because in most Latin American countries this is the norm. Schools there are far stricter than schools here in San Francisco.

Thirdly, another factor has been the lack of interest and commitment within this group. It seems that there is only interest whenever there is a trip involved. Some say that this is a good way to bring back those who have been absent. I disagree, because the lack of fellowship with the Lord and other brothers and sisters in Christ tarnishes one's spiritual walk with God. Church attendance is of utmost importance. This is where we get our spiritual food! If I were not to attend church or even Sunday School, how would I expect to grow spiritually strong? It would be like not going to college and yet expect to receive a Doctorate in Medicine just because I'm familiar with over-the-counter drugs.

This tarnish was easily seen at our Jenness Park retreat last year. Jenness Park is a Christian campground in the Sonora mountain wilderness where conferences are held every year. Everything is right there within the campgrounds: cabins, recreation areas, sanctuary, cafeteria, and even a beautiful river that runs through it. This is truly a wonderful place to come and get closer to God and other fellow Christians.

Out of a group of about 25 English young adults, only six attended church on a regular basis. And out of the rest, only one was not saved and new to the group. The rest were familiar with the group and had come out of the woodwork for this trip. What resulted was spiritual chaos. There was arguing, bad language, obscene jokes, cliques and put downs on members of the same group. We could not agree on anything because of the prevailing bad attitudes. There was not a single meal that we ate as a group. By the end of the four day weekend, the trip had become a complete nightmare.

The best thing that happened was that the new member I mentioned earlier received Christ. It's amazing how God manifests Himself even amidst complete chaos. There is always a lesson to be learned from disappointments. Having experienced Jenness last year, most of the young adults that attended this year had higher expectations and some fear.

Things went a lot smoother than last year. And, even a new thing happened that was unexpected—both English and Spanish young adults spent much of the trip together in worship and just plain fun.

We knew that it took a united effort to create a united group. Only in teamwork can one find togetherness. There is a saying I learned in the Marines while in boot camp: "There is no 'I' in the word team." I sincerely pray and hope that this is not only a phase we are going through, but instead that this may be the beginning of many beautiful memories together as one church Primera.

Spanish and English Young Adults
Last year at Jenness Park, the English Young Adults realized that

we needed a leader. It was not enough for us to organize Bible studies. We were seen as guides and peers, not as decision-makers for the group. This absence of leadership created "too many chefs in the kitchen."

In 1992 when Nestor Menjivar took the position of English Young Adult leader, we saw him as a figure of authority due to his being older than all of us. The group functioned well at that time and from those years of unity came the wonderful memories that David refers to. We not only had our weekly Bible studies, but also true fellowship.

After a few years, George Anaya took over as leader and the joy continued for the next year. Our meetings gathered 10 to 15 young adults on a weekly basis. We were all in our late teens or early twenties. Most of us were still living at home and going to college. In other words, we had no major responsibilities. Then, George got married and it soon became time for him to concentrate on his new family.

After much urging from the young adults, Mike Rodriguez accepted the idea of being George's replacement. Mike was our peer, but he was the most knowledgeable of the Bible. Therefore, we saw him as someone who could teach us about the Bible, but not as an authority figure. So it became frustrating for him to have the title of "leader," yet not be treated as one. After some months, the group began to disintegrate. It wasn't because of anything Mike did or didn't do. We just allowed silly problems to get between us and God. Sometimes it felt like we were "kids of the kingdom" instead of the Young Adults. Mike continued to teach young adults in Sunday School.

Our weekly Bible studies were never quite as organized as Obreros de la Viña. We normally "played it by ear." However, this was normal for us and it worked well during the time we were a group. We never had a Directorate, only a leader and a treasurer. Our structure was built more loosely. I believe this reflects a cultural difference between American Latinos and Latinos from our mother lands.

According to Gerry Lopez, Jenness Park Camp Committee Director, our group has reached a plateau and is on the decline. At this point, we need to assess our group and restructure, to face a rebirth or a death. I don't think any of us want death. We're at the bottom of our cycle and can only go up.

Although life changes have affected the group as a whole, the marriages, babies, careers, growing up, this should not change our relationship with our Creator. We think our ultimate goal should be to fellowship together with our newfound friends, Obreros de la Viña, and have outings at least every couple months. Together is the only way we will be able to cross our cultural borders.

4. Pathways of Ministry

Young Adult Ministry at St. Stephen Baptist Church
By Pauline Berryman

St. Stephen Baptist Church, a predominately African-American congregation, is located in La Puente, California, a suburban community about 20 minutes east of downtown Los Angeles. It is a cooperating Southern Baptist Church of 5240 members with connections to the Los Angeles Baptist Association, the California Southern Baptist Convention and the Southern Baptist Convention. Its pastor, Dr. E.W. McCall, Sr., who has led this congregation since 1970, is active in both state and national denominational life.

Pauline Berryman, a young adult herself, serves as Outreach Leader in the Young Adult Sunday School Department.

Sunday School: Extending the Pathway

St. Stephen is unique because the Sunday School is the beginning point of its ministry to people of all ages. It sees the Sunday School as an enhancement of the worship service as people connect with the church. Its growth over the years has been due in part to its pastor's, and by extension, its members' commitment to a quality Bible study time filled with aggressive and trained leaders. This church takes every opportunity it can to send its Sunday School leadership, including those from the Young Adult Department, to any local, regional, state or national training event that is offered. With 3,010 people enrolled it is one of the largest African-American, and Southern Baptist Sunday Schools in the state of California. St. Stephen is a flagship Sunday School Church.

Sunday School has become the pathway by which young adult ministries flourish in this church. Typically an active church is to involve young adults in every aspect of the church ministry. In essence, the young adult department is connected to a growth-oriented Sunday School.

The Young Adult Sunday School department has 231 on the roll with an attendance of around 75. The majority of the young adults range from 18-28 years old, but our definition of the young adult may not fit this standard age range. Many of the participants on Sunday and in the weekly young adult activities are three to five years older or younger than the defined age for this group. The young adult department has opened its door to those who feel young at heart. The idea is to minister to the churched and the non-churched regardless of their age.

Sunday School is also the core for the strength of the young adult department. A variety of activities spring from the regular Sunday School organization. You will see young adults in action as they participate in various ways. Thursday Night Bible Study, College Away Ministry, Sanctuary Choir, evangelism outreach, the annual young adult retreat, as well as Young Adult Council, Baptist Young Women and Brotherhood Ministry, are examples of some of the ministries that take place during the week and throughout the year. The church and its leaders make sure that young adults are themselves involved in the leadership and direction of those ministries.

Care and Share/Thursday Night Bible Studies
Care and Share, the event which launched the popular Thursday night Bible study, originated as a weekly meeting for young adults. It was an open forum for Young Adults to talk about issues that face them everyday. AIDS, single-parenting, pre-marital sex, finding the right mate, marriage, education, careers and American

prejudices, to name a few, were discussed openly and honestly. This was a unstructured arena to find out what the young adult department needed to put in order to be proactive in ministry. Care and Share met for less than three months because its purpose was to allow a segue to other ministries.

Thursday night Bible study was a result of Care and Share, and in the future there will be other ministries that will sprout from this forum. The Thursday night Bible study still addresses issues that face today's young adults. This event allows young adults to: 1) comprehend what God has to say regarding their lives, 2) understand what God expects of them, 3) reiterate the blessings God has in store for those who believe in His Word.

College Away Ministry

Another pathway that a young adult may take to minister is the College Away Ministry. Because college for most adults starts around age 18, many of our Sunday School members take advantage of going away to attend college outside the local area of the church. The College Away ministry was created to make sure that a great number of our young adults were not forgotten because they were not physically present. The ministry is thriving and special activities have been created to make sure they come to church during their Easter, Summer and Christmas breaks from school.

Evangelistic Outreach

The evangelism ministry within the young adult department is growing through the concentrated efforts of the Young Adult Sunday School Department, weekly Young Adult Bible Study, and the annually Young Adult Retreat. The Young Adult Sunday School department weekly extends God's Word through Sunday morning class dialogue, phone calls, visitation, postcards, rap sessions and a weekly twelve hour prayer fast. Our evangelism ministry is strongly motivated by the Great Commission of Matthew 28:19-20.

Annual Young Adult Retreat

Each year about forty young adults spend the weekend in the California mountains to develop their leadership skills, build their friendships and strengthen their relationships with Jesus Christ. They also have the opportunity in Bible study to present issues and seek His divine wisdom and power. This retreat gives them the chance to shape and mold spiritual growth through a prayerful life. The annual young adult retreat is an open invitation to the churched and the unchurched.

Leadership

St. Stephen believes in developing leadership for the future. The leadership of the church believes that we must educate, train and promote involvement in the ministry of the church. Young adults are strategically put in leadership positions to make sure growth continues. All the ministries that work for and with young adults depend on their own leadership to make things happen.

Choir

Important to an African-American church, are the choirs that are a part of the worship service each week. St. Stephen's has 4 choirs, but the young adults minister through the Sanctuary Choir, formally known as the Young Adult Choir.

Between 1972-73 God touched the heart of an aggressive young lady of St. Stephen to approach pastor E. W. McCall, Sr. with a burning desire to begin a young adult choir. Pastor McCall welcomed the ministry because he understood the need to organize and prepare young people for ministry. The young adults faced the challenge with enthusiasm, hard work and success.

The Sanctuary Choir started with about forty members. Key people in the church worked faithfully with the music department to enhance the ministry. The young adults became more excited about serving God. Soon a strong yearning for the Word of God began to erupt in the hearts and minds of those choir members. They were like David in Psalm 119:10 where he said, "I will seek you with all my heart, do not let me stray from your commands." As the members feasted on the Word, as God spoke through Pastor McCall, their strong will to know God's Word continued. These young adults experienced a rebirth in their spirit of inward and outward praise which soon became a part of the growing ministry at St. Stephen.

Currently the Sanctuary Choir is approximately 60 voices strong and rehearses on a weekly basis. The choir members range in age from 18-35 and have a mission to reach out to other churched and non-churched young adults. It takes its turn with the other church choirs singing for the Sunday morning worship services. The vibrant energy of this choir attracts young adults and creates expression through today's music. This group of young people can also be found on Sundays involved in various aspects of the Sunday School. The Young Adult Choir of St. Stephen Baptist Church grew from a choir to a Bible study, to Prison Ministry to servanthood.

Clues to Its Success

St. Stephen's ministry to young adults is successful for several reasons. First, young adults are as much a priority of the Sunday School as any other age group. Second, the church insists those who serve do so with commitment to excellence and training, and in turn provides that training. It trains its leaders. Third, young adults are challenged to be active participants in the life of this church through a variety of Sunday School related avenues, as well as leadership in those areas and an exciting choir program that actually takes regular responsibility to lead in worship. Young adults feel included and important at St. Stephen. That seems to make all the difference.

Appendix #1

Resources

The following agencies provide consultation, conversation, seminars, printed materials, audio and video tapes and Bible study curriculum for use with young adults.

College and Singles Ministries, California Southern Baptist Convention, 678 E. Shaw, Fresno, CA. 93710. Call 209/220-9533, extensions 233 and 234. email: 70423.1320@compuserve.com

Singles Ministry Resources, 127 Ninth Avenue, North, Nashville, TN, 37234. Call Tim Cleary at 615/251-2231. email: tcleary@bssb.com

National Student Ministries, Baptist Sunday School Board, 127 Ninth Avenue, North, Nashville, TN 37234. email: bhenry@bssb.com

SAM Journal, PO Box 62056, Colorado Springs, CO 80962-2056. email: to editor: wanderlu@pcisys.net

Network of Single Adult Leaders, PO Box 1600, Grand Rapids, MI 49501. email: nsl@gospelcom.net

Parties, Games and Drama Resources

Sharon Baack, Hall Hill and Joe Palmer, Adventure Recreation: An Adventure in Group Building. Nashville, TN. Convention Press, 1989.

Sharone Baack and Brad Smith, compilers, Adventure Recreation II, Nashville, TN: Convention Press, 1994.

Michael W. Capps, Screamers & Scramblers. Nashville, TN: Convention Press, 1994.

Christy M. Haines, editor, *National Drama Service: Christian Scripts for Stage, Street & Sancturary,* a subcription drama service provided by the Baptist Sunday School Board (LifeWay Christian Resources) 127 Ninth Avenue, North, Nashville, TN 37234.

Georgre Siler, Games With a Purpose. Nashville, TN: Convention Press, 1994.

Marty Sprague, Fifteen Community Builders for Young Adults. Fresno, CA: College and Singles Ministries, California Southern Baptist Convention, 1996
    Request your copy by writing to:
        College and Singles Ministries
        678 East Shaw Avenue, Fresno, CA 93710.
        (Please enclose $1 for shipping and handling.)

Tommy Yessick, compiler, Sport Ministry for Churches. Nashville, TN: Convention Press, 1995.

Web Sites of Interest to Young Adults and Those Who Minister With Them

Check them out and see what you can find!!

www.sbc.org
www.bssb.com
www.crossseekers.org
www.csbc.com
www.goshen.com
www.thegospel.com.net/nsl
www.imb.org/students/
www.namb.net/student/
www.wmu.com/wmu

Appendix #2

Suggested Topics and Issues

The following are suggestions for materials and topics for use with young adults 18-24 years of age. These topics may be used at any time young adults can be gathered, including Sunday morning. Meeting times during the week can provide opportunities for biblically based studies of topics pertinent to young adult concerns.

Curriculum-Based Studies

1. Each of the three Bible study curriculum series published by the Baptist Sunday School Board, Lifeway Christian Resources, has either age-group or life-situation group-specific material appropriate for young adult study. To receive a catalogue with the latest curriculum information call the Customer Service Division at 1-800-458-2772, or via Internet: www.bssb.com or www.bssb.com/order/index.asp.

2. Much of the BSSB Life Support Material is worth using with this group, though the time commitment demanded by the material might be a hindrance. As with all material, this could be used as a basis for study, but modified by the leader to fit the need and situation.

> *Experiencing God*
> *The Mind of Christ*
> *The Search for Significance*
> *Bible Guide to Discipleship and Doctrine*
> *Counsel for the Nearly and Newly Married*
> *I Take Thee to be My Spouse*
> *Prayer Life*

and many other titles in this series are valuable for study.

Topic-Based Studies:

Young adults have a multitude of needs. They are not afraid of hitting hard topics head on. Topics such as those listed below will both interest and attact them.

1. Dating, Courting, and Marriage Issues
2. Studies in Relationship and Communicating, as Friends, and in a Dating or Marriage Relationship.
3. Understanding the Opposite Sex
4. Finances: Budgets, getting out of Debt, Retirement Planning
5. Ethics/Morality/True Love Waits/Temptation
6. Getting Along in the Workplace
7. Relating with Parents and Other Adults/Family Relationships.
8. Hints for Living Single: Cooking, Cleaning, Ironing
9. Becoming Godly Men
10. Becoming Godly Women
11. Character Studies of Biblical Role Models for Young Adults
12. Chapter by Chapter Study of a selected book of the Bible
13. A Study of the Parables
14. A Study of the Beatitudes
15. A Study of the Sermon on the Mount
16. Topics generated by current events or problems
17. View a Christian video or movie, discuss it/directed questions by leader.
18. Find an appropriate Christian book, read and discuss it: e.g. Finding the Love of Your Life, by Neil Clark Warren. (Note: leader would probably have to read the book and then prepare or assign chapter summaries, and discussion questions. Young adults will not likely be counted on to bring the book to the study week after week.)
19. How to Know the Will of God.
20. Goal and Career Planning
21. Spiritual Growth/Experiencing God
22. Forgiveness: Of Others and Of Self
23. Loneliness
24. Fear and Anxiety
25. Dealing with Bitterness/Anger/Rejection
26. What are the Boundaries?
27. Spiritual Gifts

Appendix #3

Outreach Ideas
by David Love

Basic Principles for Successful Outreach

1. Demonstrate concern, care and interest in young adults and their needs. Make a conscious, intentional effort to meet visitors to Sunday School and other meetings and become friends. Encourage group members to develop relationships with non-believers. Remember that people are more important than programs.

2. Develop and maintain a well-rounded ministry plan that includes Bible study, fellowship, evangelism, leadership training, missions, and G.O.F. *(Good Old Fun)*. Remember that variety offers more opportunity, and that the more hooks you use, the better chance you have to catch a fish. *(Especially if you fish in a stocked pond.)*

3. Encourage in your young adults the habits of prayer, quiet time and Bible Study. When we are primarily interested in a person coming to "know Christ" (relationship) rather than in a person coming to "something" (religious activity) people will respond. As we "know Christ" our passion and compassion increase.

Characteristics of Successful Outreach

1. Outreach must be personal to be successful. Do not rely on posters, bulk mailings or gimmicks.

2. Outreach begins with the leader, but heavily depends upon the followers. Leaders set the pace.

3. Outreach should be an aspect of everything we do. Make it easy for people to get involved. Always ask, "How does this activity promote outreach?"

4. For outreach to have any permanent effect, it must be geared to meeting individual needs and giving opportunity for meaningful involvement.

5. Seek "excellence" in the quality of outreach endeavors.

6. A commitment to grow is a commitment to being uncomfortable some of the time.

7. Follow-up is always made.

Ideas For Outreach/Fellowship

1. *Information Table on a Local College Campus*
Target the best time of year (beginning of quarter/semester) for special outreach activity, but do not neglect the rest of the year. The value of consistent visibility is immense.

Make the table as attractive as possible. (Excellence)

Locate in the most trafficked areas.

Don't just sit behind the table.

Use give a-ways.

> *Tapes:* Firefighters for Christ, 8866 Barcelona Plaza, Westminister, CA 92683

> *Tracts:* C.S.B.C. Evangelism Department,
> 678 E. Shaw, Fresno, CA 93710.
> A variety of tracts are available for purchase at a low cost.

Occasionally do something crazy, out of the ordinary:
Cookie For Your Thoughts
Unbirthday Bash

2. *Outreach Special Events*
Use events in which your target group is interested.

Make it easy to attend.

Emphasize "Contact Consciousness" with leaders.

Use activities that allow smaller groups to be used at some point. It is hard to connect in a crowd.

Factors that must be considered: location, length of time, date, cost, interest, space needed, transportation required, props, purpose of event, etc.

Be creative and bold. If it works, improve it. If it doesn't, toss it. If you're not sure, try it.

3. *Fellowship Events*
"Friends Becoming Family"
Goals:
(1) to involve participants in getting to know one another.
(2) to offer encouraging, wholesome fun.
(3) to communicate Christian love and caring through actions and words.

Fellowship Ideas:
    —Seasonal Events—Table Game Night-Progressive Dinner—Scavenger Hunts—Theme Fellowships
    —Sports Events
    —Video Nights—Roller-skating—Out of town trips to amusement parks-state or regional young adult retreats.

Let leaders decide events. Be slow to use your "veto power" but don't hesitate if you must.

4. *Ideas for Missions*

Community/Campus Service Projects:
Survival Kits (Beginning of school or finals/to celebrate new apartments or life changes.) Include staples, sweet treats, fruit/nuts, pencils, dryer sheets, etc. Include an appropriate tract, church brochure or New Testament.
Adopt-A-Grandparent
Community Programs: Big Brothers/Big Sisters, Tutoring
Food drives at Thanksgiving/Christmas or serving in a food ministry.
Habitat for Humanity

Short-term (for a few weeks, a semester or the summer) Volulnteer Missions:
Church Summer Youth Directors/Camp Staff
Denominational, or other agency volunteer missions programs.

Prayer Ministry: Prayer Partners, Prayer Events, Prayer Retreats.

Bibliography

Books

Adler, Mortimer J., and Charles Van Doren. How to Read a Book: The Classic Guide to Intelligent Reading. New York: Simon and Schuster, 1972.

Ahlstrom, Sidney E. A Religious History of the American People. New Haven, CN: Yale University Press, 1972.

Atkinson, Harley, ed. Handbook of Young Adult Religious Education. Birmingham, AL: Religious Education Press, 1995.

Bantz, Jeffrey R. Generation X: Implications for Missions Organizations of the Sociological Distinctives of Chritsians Born Between 1961 and 1975. Miami, FL: Latin American Mission, 1995.

Barna, George. Generation Next: What You Need to Know About Today's Youth. Ventura, CA: Regal Books, 1995.

_____. The Invisible Generation: Baby Busters. Glendale, CA: Barna Research, 1992.

Baugh, Ken. A Guide to Understanding Generation X Sub-Cultures. McLean, VA: Frontline Ministry Resources, 1996.

Best, Harold M. Music Through the Eyes of Faith. San Francisco, CA: Harper San Franciscio, 1993.

Celek, Tim, and Dieter Zander. Inside the Soul of a New Generation: Insights and Strategies for Reaching Busters. Grand Rapids, MI: Zondervan Publishing House, 1996.

Chickering, Arthur W. Education and Identity. San Francisco, CA: Jossey-Bass, Inc. Publishers, 1969.

Chinn, Wilberta. Singles Sorting It Out. Whittier, CA: Peacock Enterprises, 1991.

Cohen, Jason, and Michael Krugman. Generation ECCH!: The Backlash Starts Here. New York: Simon and Schuster, 1994.

Coupland, Douglas. Life After God. New York: Pocket Books, 1994.

Erikson, Erik. Childhood and Society. Second Edition. New York: W.W. Norton & Company, Inc., 1963.

Fagerstrom, Douglas, ed. Singles' Ministry Handbook. Wheaton, IL: Victor Books, 1989.

_____, ed. Single Adult Ministry: The Next Step. Wheaton, IL: Victor Books, 1993.

Ford, Kevin Graham. Jesus for a New Generation: Putting the Gospel in the Language of Xers. Downers Grove, IL: InterVarsity Press, 1995.

Ford, Leighton, with James Denney. The Power of Story: Rediscovering the Oldest, Most Natural Way to Reach People for Christ. Colorado Springs, CO: NavPress, 1994.

Fowler, James W. Becoming Adult, Becoming Christian. San Francisco, CA: Harper and Row, 1984.

_____. Stages Of Faith. San Francisco, CA: Harper and Row, 1981.

_____. Weaving The New Creation. San Francisco, CA: Harper and Row, 1991.

Gallup, George, Jr., and Robert Bezilla The Religious Life of Young Americans. Princeton, NJ: The George Gallup International Institute, 1992.

Garber, Julie, ed. Ministry With Young Adults: The Search for Intimacy. Elgin, IL: FaithQuest, the trade imprint of Brethren Press, 1992.

Gribbon, Clifford T. Developing Faith In Young Adults: Effective Ministry With 18-35 Year Olds. New York: The Alban Institute, 1990.

Hanks, Louis B. Vision, Variety, and Vitality: Teaching Today's Adult Generations. Nashville, TN: Convention Press, 1996.

Harrison, Dan, with Gordon Aeschliman. Romancing the Globe: The Call of the Wild on Generation X. Downers Grove, IL: InterVarsity Press, 1993.

Herron, Art. Ministering to Students Through the Church. Nashville, TN: Convention Press, 1989.

Hersey, Terry, et al. Giving the Ministry Away. Elgin, IL: David C. Cook Publishing Co.,1993 .

Hersey, Terry. Young Adult Ministry. Loveland, CO: Group Books, 1986.

Howe, Neil, and Bill Strauss. 13th Gen: Abort. Retry. Ignore. Fail? New York: Vintage Books, 1993.

Jones, Jerry, ed. Growing Your Single Adult Ministry. Colorado Springs, CO: Cook Ministry Resources, 1993.

Koons, Carolyn A., and Michael J. Anthony. Single Adult Passages: Uncharted Territory. Grand Rapids, MI: Baker Book House, 1991.

LeFever, Marlene D. Learning Styles: Reaching Everyone God Gave You To Teach. Colorado Springs, CO: David C. Cook, 1995.

Littwin, Susan. The Postponed Generation: Why American Youths Are Growing Up Later, New York: William Morrow, 1986.

Loeb, Paul Rogat. Generation at the Crossroads: Apathy and Action on the American Campus. New Brunswick, NJ: Rutgers University Press, 1994.

Long, Jimmy. Generation Hope: A Strategy for Reaching the Post Modern Generation. Downers Grover, IL: InterVarsity Press, 1997

Mahedy, William, and Janet Bernardi. A Generation Alone: Xers Making a Place in the World. Downers Grove, IL: InterVarsity Press, 1994.

McDowell, Josh, and Bob Hostetler. Right from Wrong: What You Need to Know to Help Youth Make Right Choices. Dallas, TX: Word Publishing Company, 1994.

McIntosh, Gary L. Three Generations: Riding theWaves of Change in Your Church. Grand Rapids, MI: Fleming H. Revell, 1995.

Miller, Craig Kennet. Post-Moderns: The Beliefs, Hopes & Fears of Young Americans (1965-1981). Nashville, TN: Discipleship Resources, 1996.

Nilson, Sue and Andy Morgan. Starting A Single Adult Ministry.Colorado Springs, CO: David C.Cook Publishing Co., 1994.

Raines, Claire, and Lawrence Bradford. Twenty Something: Managing And Motivating Today's New Work Force. New York: Master Media Limited, 1992.

Ritchie, Karen. Marketing to Generation X. New York: Lexington Books, 1995.

Rydberg, Denny. Twentysomething: Life Beyond College. Grand Rapids, MI: Zondervan Publishing House, 1991.

Roxburg, Alan J. Reaching a New Generation: Strategies for Tomorrow's Church. Downers Grove, IL: InterVarsity Press, 1993.

Schultze, Quentin K. et al., Dancing In the Dark. Grand Rapids, MI: Eerdmans, 1991.

Sloan-Collier, Kay. Single In The Church: New Ways to Minister With 52 Percent Of God's People. New York: The Alban Institute, 1992.

Strauss, William, and Neil Howe, Generations: A History Of American's Future. 1584-2069. New York: William Morrow, 1991.

The Forgotten Half: Pathways To Success For America's Youth And Young Families. By Harold Howe II, Chairperson. New York: The William T. Grant Foundation Commission on Work, Family, and Citizenship, 1988.

Tillman, William M., Jr. AIDS: A Christian Reponse. Nashville, TN: Convention Press, 1990.

Tulgan, Bruce. Managing Generation X: How to Bring Out the Best in Young Talent. Santa Monica, CA: Merritt Publishing, 1995.

Walker, Williston. A History of the Christian Church. 4th ed. New York: Charles Scribners' Sons, 1985.

Yount, William R. Created to Learn: A Christian Teacher's Introduction to Educational Psychology. Nashville, TN: Broadman and Holman, Publishers, 1996.

Zustiak, Gary. The NeXt Generation: Understanding and Meeting the Needs of Generation X. Joplin, MO: College Press Publishing Company, 1996.

Articles

"alt.ministry@gen.X.forum." NEXT, 2: (April 1996), 1.

Ford, Keven Graham. "My So-Called Generation: A Buster Speaks." The Ivy Jungle Report, 4 (Fall 1995): 8.

Giles, Jeff. "Generalizations X." Newsweek, 6 June 1994, 66.

Harteis, Eirik Frederick. "Theme for Generation X." Sojourners, November 1994, 19.

Hornblower, Margot, "Great Xpectations." Time, June 9, 1997, 149:23, 58-69.

Jones, Kent. "The Spin: talkin' 'bout our generation." Seventeen, August 1993, 131-132.

Kerbel, Jarrett et al. "Generation's Faith." Sojourners, November 1994, 15-20.

Ludwig, Robert. "Twentysomethings: Struggling to Find a Meaningful Life." The Catholic World 238:1427(September/October 1995), 197.

Sontag, Marie. "More Sex, Less Intimacy." Youthworker VI:1 (Summer 1989): 43-40.

Verteufeuille, John. "Lowering the Odds of Sexual Promiscuity." Youthworker VI:1 (Summer 1989), 36-37.

Zander, Dieter, "Baby Busters: How to Reach a New Generation." Pastor's Update Listening Guide, Fuller Evangelistic Association, November, 1992.

_____ "The Gospel for Generation X." Leadership XVI:2 (Spring 1995), 37.

Order Form

Please complete both address sections.

```
┌─────────────────────────────────────────────────┐
│           Address Label - please print clearly!  │
│   Name _____   │
│   Address _____   │
│   _____St. _____Zip _____  │
└─────────────────────────────────────────────────┘
```

Name _____

Address _____

_____

State _____ Zip _____

Please send me_____copy(ies) of your book,
Intersecting Lives: Road Maps for Ministry with Young Adults

I am enclosing $_____ to cover the cost of the
purchase of the book and shipping and handling.

Send cash, check or money order and this completed form to:
WILLOW CITY PRESS
678 East Shaw Avenue
Fresno, California 93710

_____ Books at $11.00 each   = _____
(California sales tax included in book price)

Shipping and handling at $2.00 per book_____ =

Total   = _____
Please make check or money
order payable to CSBC

OFFICE USE ONLY
Date received: _____
Date order sent: _____

WILLOW CITY PRESS
is a ministry of the Church Growth Division of the California Southern Baptist Convention